For Laurel,
You inspire women to solve

SOLVING FOR X
IN THE Y DOMAIN

Strategies for Overcoming
Gender Barriers to Leadership

For X in all domains! Keep up the great work,
Gae
11/25/24

Gae Walters, PhD

ARCHWAY
PUBLISHING

This book is a work of non-fiction. Unless otherwise noted, the author
and the publisher make no explicit guarantees as to the accuracy of
the information contained in this book and in some cases, names of
people and places have been altered to protect their privacy.

Archway Publishing books may be ordered through booksellers or by contacting:

Archway Publishing
1663 Liberty Drive
Bloomington, IN 47403
www.archwaypublishing.com
1 (888) 242-5904

Because of the dynamic nature of the Internet, any web addresses or links contained in
this book may have changed since publication and may no longer be valid. The views
expressed in this work are solely those of the author and do not necessarily reflect the
views of the publisher, and the publisher hereby disclaims any responsibility for them.

Any people depicted in stock imagery provided by Thinkstock are models,
and such images are being used for illustrative purposes only.
Certain stock imagery © Thinkstock.

ISBN: 978-1-4808-5270-9 (sc)
ISBN: 978-1-4808-5269-3 (hc)
ISBN: 978-1-4808-5271-6 (e)

Library of Congress Control Number: 2017917885

Print information available on the last page.

Archway Publishing rev. date: 11/28/2017

Daniel K. Dayton, PhD
Professor, The Chicago School of Professional Psychology
ddayton@thechicagoschool.edu

Subject: Recommendation: 2015 Emerald/EFMD Outstanding Doctoral
Research Awards

Dear Review Committee Members:

It is with humble honor and great pleasure that I support the nomination of Gae Walters' dissertation study, Solving for X in the Y Domain:
Overcoming Gender-Based Barriers to Leadership. Dr. Walters has
completed a "first of its kind" extensive phenomenological study of the
experiences of senior-level and executive-level women leaders in a wide
range of fields in science, technology, engineering, and mathematics in
overcoming gender bias.

These fields have traditionally been dominated by males, and in
spite of the forces of social change efforts to open these fields to women,
that male-dominated paradigm continues to exist today. Social change
efforts have concentrated on altering the forces of male hegemony, gender bias, gender backlash, gendered cultures, and buffering behaviors
to overcome the issue of male dominance, but have not encountered
significant success.

Deep-seated and often hidden cultural and psychological paradigms operate to thwart change efforts, perhaps because the dominant
male leaders in STEM fields are unaware of the female perspective of
those paradigms.

**For the first time, this study enlightens a female perspective
of the forces, issues, paradigms, and behaviors that women face
when aspiring to leadership positions. Dr. Walters' research, exceptionally well supported by theoretical constructs that provide
multi-dimensional perspectives for analyzing and understanding the perspective of the lived experiences of women who have**

overcome those barriers, provides remarkably fresh insight to overcoming those forces. The inductive construction of that understanding, built from the phenomenological analysis of the participant's lived experiences, establishes a viable framework for finally developing potentially generalized strategies for gender neutrality ... and equality ... in leadership in the male-dominated fields.

Dr. Walters' research is exceptional in its thoroughness, its insight, its analysis, and in its originality. Moreover, the potential contribution of Dr. Walters' research to future study and future practical application is unmistakable. Any woman who reads this study is likely to be nodding in recognition and agreement to her findings and conclusions. Any man who reads the study is likely to experience moments of epiphany at the exposure of hidden paradigms that dominate STEM culture. Not only is Dr. Walters' study scientifically compelling, it is also socially compelling on many different levels. In my humble opinion, Dr. Walters' study deserves international recognition for its incisiveness, originality, and its potential impact. I heartily support its nomination for the 2015 Emerald/EFMD Outstanding Doctoral Research Awards.

To: Gae Walters, PhD

"This work is elegant and compelling. Thinking from the perspective/ values of ancient Greek philosophy, I experienced reverence for beauty and truth in this study. I have no doubt that goodness will follow when the lessons are brought to women in STEM leadership. I hope you and Dr. Dayton, so close to this work, do not take its quality for granted; both of you deserve loud applause and gratitude from the Organizational Leadership faculty and students.

I found the descriptions of the experience to be robust and detailed; sometimes, I felt shock. I may not want women want to hear but the shameless comments from men stunned me. **Rather than continuing to describe the disease and wringing hands you are choosing to study positive deviants ... women who did not wait to be empowered, who did not rely on the organizations to remove the structural barriers to advancement but took it on themselves to act -- and succeeded."**

Loved the expressions (Mother Theresa and Madame Curie; the more important the meeting, the higher the heels, etc.) and really appreciated the quality of the writing, which is critical for phenomenology. I come away from this with a deeper appreciation for the experience and women leaders themselves. Plus, you have taught me, you have 'sophisticated my beholding' of the everyday world of women leaders at work. I discovered some of my own unconscious bias toward women in leadership and felt embarrassed but not shamed. There was no sermonizing; the facts were damning."

Martin J. Leahy, Ph.D.
Professor, PhD Organizational Leadership program
Chair, National Faculty Council
The Chicago School of Professional Psychology

DEDICATION

With deep gratitude to the women who shared their stories of struggle, perseverance, and success … you showed us how to solve for X in the Y domain.

To all my dear sisters,
Claim your scepters
Unsheathe your grit
Some fortress walls
Were made to be scaled
Some castle balls
Were meant to be crashed
And there are kingdoms full of men
That need saving
Palaces with hibernating princes
That beg to be stirred
So open their eyes
Show them there is more than one way
To skin a dragon
That much in this world
Is more mighty than a sword
And you've got brains
More swift than any arrow
You've got vision
Sharper than any spear
And your dreams have the power
To transform empires
Just breathe in
Fill your lungs
Set your voice free
And repeat:
Happily ever after
Begins with me.

CONTENTS

LIST OF FIGURES

LIST OF TABLES

PREFACE

The purpose of this feminist phenomenological study is to capture and describe the experiences of women leaders in male-dominated professions who have used buffering behaviors to overcome gender-based barriers to career advancement. This study is set within the framework of Bandura's social cognitive theory, which holds that an individual can consciously learn and choose behaviors that will influence outcomes within their environments. Two aspects of social cognitive theory, self-regulation and self-efficacy, are central to the study. This study showed that strategies and behaviors exist that women can utilize to overcome the pervasive gender-based barriers to leadership frequently encountered in the fields of science, technology, engineering, and mathematics. Foundational to one's ability to apply these mitigating mechanisms known as buffering behaviors is a strong sense of self-efficacy, which developed for the women in this study early in life. The implications of these findings suggest that in addition to providing access and encouragement for young girls to study science, technology, engineering, and mathematics, messages and experiences that develop self-efficacy and the development of buffering behaviors are essential.

ACKNOWLEDGMENTS

One looks back with appreciation to the brilliant teachers,
but with gratitude to those who touched our human feelings.

—Carl Jung

As I look back on this doctoral journey, I recognize how extremely privileged I was to have been guided by brilliant teachers who also touched human feelings. A dissertation is conceived, designed, and constructed on a solid but often unheralded foundation consisting of an extensive support system. This dissertation is complete because of the commitment, collaboration, and brilliant teaching of Dr. Julie Benesh, Dr. Daniel Dayton, and Dr. Martin Leahy, my committee members, and the positive encouragement I received from a legion of others.

Specifically ...

To Dr. Daniel Dayton, the chair of my dissertation committee, you expressed the utmost confidence in me, treated me as a colleague, championed my research approach, encouraged me to think independently, and provided the space for me to go far beyond what I imagined possible.

To Dr. Julie Benesh, you reached out to me early in the program and transformed my anxiety to excitement as you guided my learning, expanded my thinking, and enriched my ideas. I will always be grateful for your counsel, your accessibility, and your feedback. You maintained a constant interest in my progress, and I sincerely thank you for broadening my intellectual horizons and setting me on a course of inquiry that has enriched my life.

To Dr. Martin Leahy, a master teacher, you were always so generous with your time and your knowledge. You introduced me to the beauty and richness of the human story through phenomenology, and you exquisitely modeled the art of being present. Your perspective helped the story unfold as you introduced me to the wonderful world of positive deviants.

To Nicky and Larry, thank you for being there unconditionally throughout this entire process and for being my steadfast sentinels, providing a safe and quiet sanctuary to which I could escape to read, to think, and to write … and for never questioning my reasons or my sanity.

To Andrea Dianni, you ran interference on my behalf, organized and supervised our practice, kept clients informed and happy, and were always there when I needed you most. I truly could not have done this without you. To Carter Manucy, my IT guru, you magically recovered lost documents, restored crashed programs, and always remained calm, cool, and confident as you spent countless hours finding what I had lost, including my mind.

Special thanks go to Kevin Schwandt, my NCADE dissertation writing expert who guided me through the unfamiliar maze of the dissertation process, provided thorough reviews of my manuscript, and generously shared ideas about its improvement.

I also thank the many outstanding faculty members of the Chicago School of Professional Psychology who encouraged my learning, fostered my passion for research, and enriched my doctoral experience—Dr. Randall Chang, Dr. Robert Gramillano, Dr. Sherri Hill, Dr. Katy Kleinfeldt, Dr. Kimberly Long, Dr. Jack McClure, Dr. Kate Noone, and my very first professor at TCS, the delightful Jennifer Cooley. I am deeply grateful to each of you for your confidence in me and for your commitment to my learning.

My far-flung family has been a constant source of strength, inspiration, and love. To the cheering Chelsea clan, the devoted denizens of Denver, and the bedazzling Bartow bevy, I am indebted to all of you for providing immense encouragement, colossal love, and steadfast support.

I add special and personal thanks to Amy Atwell and Andrea Sexton, the crown princesses of study buddies. You always made sure there were equal measures of laughter and learning! To Dr. Mary Senne, you blazed the trail and showed me what was possible. Thanks to all of you for your camaraderie, warmth, and friendship.

And most of all, I thank and honor my parents, Phyllis Escovitz Walters and William Ellsworth Walters, for their unwavering belief in me and for the sacrifices they made to ensure I had the most amazing opportunities to grow and to learn and to cultivate my curiosity. Like so many of the participants in this study, I owe my beliefs of self-efficacy to them. I know they would be proud—but not surprised.

Introduction

Background of the Problem

Women have made significant strides in climbing the corporate ladder (Bowles 2012; Evans 2010), dismantling the glass ceiling (Hymnowitz and Schellhardt 1986; Barreto, Ryan, and Schmitt 2009; Smith, Caputi, and Crittenden 2012) and navigating the labyrinth of leadership (Barsh and Yee 2011; Eagly and Carli 2007). Yet the advancement of significant numbers of women to senior leadership has been exceedingly slow. As aspiring women strive to reach the senior executive levels of organizations, they encounter numerous barriers (Brescoll, Dawson, and Uhlmann 2010; Reinhold 2005; Rose and Thomas 2009). Qualified women still do not hold senior executive positions in the same relative proportion as men, even though significant numbers of women are in midlevel management, a source of potential leaders (Desvaux, Devillard, and Sancier-Sultan 2010; Weyer 2007; Sörlin et al. 2011). Women are also significantly underrepresented on corporate boards where executive appointments are usually made (Vinnicombe 2011; Zajac and Westphal 1996).

Female leaders in the traditionally male professions of science, technology, engineering, and mathematics (STEM) are particularly scarce, and their route to senior leadership is even more arduous (Catalyst 2013; Fox and Colatrella 2006; Wentling and Thomas 2007). Women with advanced degrees in the STEM disciplines represent a candidate pool of potential leaders with exceptional competencies and strong educational backgrounds (Hewlett et al. 2008; Hill, Corbett, and St. Rose 2010). Even though more women are attaining advanced degrees in science, technology, engineering, and mathematics, the percentage of women in leadership in science and engineering remains minimal (Fox and Colatrella 2006; Hewlett et al. 2008; Lemons and Parzinger 2007; Wentling and Thomas 2009) and the underrepresentation of women in senior leadership persists (Barsh and Yee 2011; Hill, Corbett, and St. Rose 2010; Simmons, Duffy, and Alfraih 2012).

In 2012, women held approximately 14 percent of the senior executive positions in Fortune 500 companies as compared to approximately 85 percent for men; the percentage of women drops to less than 5 percent at the CEO level (Soares 2012). As recently as 2013, no women held executive positions in over half of S&P 100 companies, including Apple Computer, Kellogg, Delta Airlines, Costco Wholesale, Whirlpool, and General Mills (DeGroot, Mohapatra, and Lippmann 2013). In the fields of science, technology, engineering, and mathematics, the statistics are even more troubling (Buck Luce et al. 2008; Bureau of Labor Statistics Current Population Survey 2012; Soe and Yakura 2008; Wentling and Thomas 2007). According to the US Department of Labor Statistics Population Survey of 2012, women working STEM professions are working in lower-level technical support roles (Catalyst 2013; Ceci and Williams 2010; Soe and Yakura 2008).

And yet many women persevere in their quest to become senior leaders. Increasingly, albeit in small numbers, women have overcome the forces that have prevented qualified women from entering the executive suites of corporations (Bowles 2012; Matsa and Miller 2011; Watts 2009; Wentling and Thomas 2009). The CEOs of General Motors, Hewlett Packard, IBM, Lockheed Martin, and PepsiCo Inc. are now women (Catalyst 2014). However, very little is known about the experience of overcoming gendered obstacles and reaching senior executive roles, particularly in male-dominated STEM fields. The goal of this phenomenological study is to discover from the experiences of women who are leaders in these fields the essence of the experience of overcoming gender-based barriers to reach senior-level leadership positions in their organizations, and the hope is to share these insights and skills with other aspiring women.

This study focused on the women who have succeeded in the male-dominated STEM fields and who have learned from their journeys. Studies of women who have achieved senior executive positions (Bowles 2012; Luster 2011; Madsen 2006) illustrate the importance of describing the lived experiences of women who have sought senior leadership positions and succeeded. Chapter 1 describes the background of the problem and the significance of the study. Also presented are the theoretical perspectives and the conceptual framework that were used to investigate the phenomenon and the central research question. The chapter concludes with explanations of the terminology and a discussion of the assumptions, limitations, and delimitations of the study. The research presented throughout the chapter supports the need for the study and examines data that illustrates the background of the problem.

Authors of a Catalyst study entitled "Bit by Bit: Advancing Women in High Tech Companies" found that the career-advancement barriers to women that both men and women reported most frequently included the lack of acceptance of women in a masculine STEM culture, isolation, and an old boys' network (Ceci and Williams 2010; Hewlett et al. 2008; Hill et al. 2010; Page, Bailey, and VanDelinder 2009). Women in Fortune 500 STEM companies hold fewer than 11 percent of executive leadership positions, a significantly lower percentage of women leaders than found in non-STEM Fortune 500 companies (Catalyst 2012).

Title VII of the Civil Rights Act of 1964 and the Equal Pay Act of 1963 opened many previously closed doors to women and minorities.

As a result, diversity in corporate employee populations is more common than ever before, but not at all levels of the organization (Acker 2006; Barreto, Ryan, and Schmitt 2009; Catalyst 2013; D'Agostino and Levine 2009; Hill et al. 2010). Barriers to the executive suite still exist for many qualified candidates. Diversity is not widespread in the management ranks and practically disappears at the executive level (Huppke 2013; Monroe et al. 2008).

For many years, the pipeline problem was blamed for the scarcity of women executives in STEM organizations or for the lack of women in middle management eligible for promotion (Ceci and Williams 2010; Soe and Yakura 2008). That no longer appears to be a valid reason. As of 2012, women held over 50 percent of the management positions in STEM organizations (Bureau of Labor Statistics Current Population Survey 2012). Another reason often given for the underrepresentation of women in senior executive positions is that women choose to place family obligations over career opportunities (Barreto, Ryan, and Schmitt 2009; Ceci and Williams 2010; Hill, Corbett, and St. Rose 2010). However, in a study of managers who were rated as promotable in the health-care/science field, women were promoted significantly less often, even after controlling for the variable of family obligations (Hopkins, O'Neil, and Bilimoria 2006).

Problem Statement

In corporate organizations, government, and society, there is a problem related to the underrepresentation of women in senior leadership ranks, particularly in the fields of science, technology, engineering, and mathematics. Despite the fact that it has been proven that women in leadership positions contribute significantly to organizational, project, and team success, their upward progress is frequently blocked (Hewlett et al. 2008; Wentling and Thomas 2007). This problem affects both organizations and people because it limits access to available talent and thought processes. Organizations need a broad array of insights, experiences, and knowledge at the senior executive level where strategic decisions and corporate direction are determined. Global competition, especially in science and technology, is rapidly growing, and corporate entities are under increasing pressure to produce innovative products and financial results (Hewlett et al. 2008). Despite the fact that many women possess the skill, knowledge, and expertise to lead (Barker, Mancha, and Ashcraft 2014; Barsh and Yee 2011; Evans 2010; Hopkins, O'Neil, and Bilimoria 2006), are innovative problem solvers (Horwitz and Horwitz 2007; Rose and Thomas 2009), and make exceptional contributions to the bottom line (Jalbert, Jalbert, and Furumo 2013; Welbourne, Cycyota, and Ferrante 2007), they continue to encounter gender-based barriers to their upward mobility (Chen, Roy, and Crawford 2010; Hewlett et al. 2008; Pai and Vaidya 2009).

There are many possible factors contributing to this problem. Gender disparity in senior leadership often stems from the fact that women who behave in ways that are viewed as counterstereotypical (e.g., assertive, competitive, and dominant) are sanctioned for violating female stereotypes of supportiveness, submissiveness, and interpersonal sensitivity (Eagly and Karau 2002; Gupta 2013; Heilman et al. 2004). Heilman's lack-of-fit model (2001), Eagly and Karau's congruity theory of prejudice (2002), and Rudman's status incongruity hypothesis (2012) support this view. Of all the negative forces that women encounter, perhaps the most pernicious is gender backlash (Garcia-Retamero and Lopez-Zafra 2006; Heilman et al. 2004; O'Neill and O'Reilly 2011). The status incongruity hypothesis (SIH) asserts that when women behave in ways that defy female gender stereotypes, they will encounter the backlash effect and be sanctioned professionally, economically, interpersonally, and socially. These sanctions include women not being hired, promoted, or included in senior decision-making forums (Eagly and Karau 2002; Gupta 2013; O'Neill and O'Reilly 2011; Rudman et al. 2012; Rudman and Phelan 2008).

The research on gender disparity, bias, and backlash in organizations is extensive; however, the focus of the research has been primarily on organizational factors such as lack of flex time, absence of mentors, stereotypical gender-based thinking, and entrenched male-dominated leadership networks (Acker 2006; Barreto, Ryan, and Schmit 2009; Carli and Eagly 2007; Ceci and Williams 2010; Connell and Messerschmidt 2005; Eagly and Karau 2002; Heilman 2001; Heilman et al. 2004; Koenig et al. 2011; Lemons and Parzinger 2007; Ridgeway 2009; Rudman et al. 2012; Sikdar and Mitra 2009). However, recent studies have shown that certain behaviors and approaches attenuate backlash reactions against women who exhibit counterstereotypical behavior (Gupta 2013; Moss-Racusin and Rudman 2010; O'Neill and O'Reilly 2011). There appear to be certain buffering behaviors that allow women to utilize counterstereotypical agentic behavior without experiencing a backlash response (Cech et al. 2011; Hirshfield 2011; Hopkins, O'Neil, and Bilimoria 2006; Kelsey 2007; O'Neill and O'Reilly 2011; Shaughnessy et al. 2011). These buffering behaviors include, but are not limited to, self-monitoring (O'Neill and O'Reilly 2011; Gupta 2013), impression management (Hirshfield 2011; O'Neill and O'Reilly 2011), political skill (Shaughnessy et al. 2011), and performance (Jalbert, Jalbert, and Furumo 2013; Welbourne, Cycyota, and Ferrante 2007).

This study adds a new dimension to the body of knowledge by providing insight and understanding of the experience of using strategies, behaviors, and skills to overcome gender bias and backlash and to reach senior leadership positions. The lived experiences of women who have overcome gender bias could provide successful strategies for other women striving to achieve senior leadership positions in male-dominated fields and lead to needed social change (Brooks & Nagy Hesse-Biber 2007). This study fills a gap in the literature by shifting the focus from external factors of gender discrimination to the experiences of the extraordinary women who have overcome the barriers found in educational systems and organizational cultures and attained senior levels of leadership (Bowles 2012).

Purpose of the Study

The purpose of this feminist phenomenological study was to discover from the lived experiences of women who are leaders in the fields of science, technology, engineering, and mathematics (STEM) the essence of the experience of using strategies, behaviors, and skills, known as buffering behaviors (Gupta 2013; Hirshfield 2011; O'Neill & O'Reilly 2011; Shaughnessy, Treadway, Breland, Williams, & Brouer 2011) to overcome gender-based barriers to reach senior-level leadership positions in their organizations. The goal is to provide insight and understanding into the experiences of women who have overcome gender discrimination and attained executive leadership roles. *Buffering behaviors* are defined as the self-monitoring skills and strategies that utilize knowledge of political behavior, impression management, and performance to overcome the gender bias and backlash women often experience when behaving in counterstereotypical ways. Gender bias and backlash were explored through the framework of the status incongruity hypothesis (SIH) which maintains that women are expected to behave in certain gender congruent ways, and when they disregard feminine gender stereotypes, they often encounter a punishing backlash effect (Eagly & Karau 2002; O'Neill & O'Reilly 2011; Rudman, Moss-Racusin, Phelan & Nauts 2012; Rudman & Phelan 2008). Bandura's social cognitive theory holds that human beings are capable of formulating and enacting planned behavior to affect outcomes and forms the basis of the study of women who have employed buffering behaviors to achieve senior leadership roles (Bandura 2001).

A phenomenological approach is appropriate for this study as it recognizes and honors the legitimacy of the human experience to provide insight and understanding into the themes of shared occurrences

(Groenewald 2004; van Manen 1984). A phenomenological exploration of gender discrimination and the strategies women have used to overcome these obstacles could offer guidance and hope to women who seek to serve in a leadership capacity in organizations (Ehrich 2005). The phenomenologist believes that understanding comes from the stories of the individuals who have experienced a phenomenon and are willing to share those insights with the rest of us (Gibson & Hanes 2003). It is through these human experiences and stories that researchers discover the essence of lived truth (Gibson & Hanes 2003; Whiting 2002).

This study also incorporates a critical theory paradigm that allows the researcher to question the current realities to work toward democratic change (Ponterotto 2005). Critical advocacy studies endeavor to make heard voices that have previously been censored or suppressed. Both critical advocacy and feminist theories examine conditions that lead to social and economic inequality, and both advocate for system change (Martin 2003). The synergies of these two theories will provide clear direction for understanding the experiences of women who have struggled with the disparity of power based on gender (Martin 2003).

Significance of the Study

There is a gap in the leadership literature regarding the lived experiences of senior women executives who have successfully overcome gender bias and backlash in male-dominated professions. A great deal has been written about the organizational and societal barriers to women who seek leadership. Much less is known about those women who did not rely on the organization to remove the structural barriers to advancement but took it upon themselves to act upon the environment and find ways to reach senior leadership positions. This is the significance of the study. This study sought to discover the essence of the experience of using self-monitoring strategies, impression management, political skill, and performance to counteract gender bias and provide successful strategies for other women striving to achieve senior leadership positions in male-dominated fields.

The literature clearly indicates the prevalence of gender disparity across male-dominated organizations such as STEM (Hewlett, Buck Luce, Servon, Sherbin, Shiller, & Sumberg 2008; Wentling & Thomas 2007). Even though more women than ever before are graduated with advanced degrees in science, technology, engineering, and mathematics, the number of women in leadership positions in these fields continues to be extremely low (Fox & Colatrella 2006; Hewlett, Buck Luce, Servon, Sherbin, Shiller, & Sumberg 2008).

There exists empirical evidence of the value of diverse teams (Herring 2009; Horwitz & Horwitz 2007; Watson, Kumar, & Michaelsen 1993) and yet leadership teams in organizations continue to lack diverse representation. A study of 506 US for-profit organizations showed a direct and positive correlation between sales revenues, customer growth, and market share with gender diversity (Herring 2009; Jalbert, Jalbert, & Furumo 2013).

The National Council of Women in Technology found that when diverse groups design IT solutions, the solutions are more successful because the needs of a wider constituent group are usually sought and incorporated into the final design (Rose & Thomas 2009). STEM organizations whose clients are in the government sectors are required to show evidence of team diversity in order to be eligible for multimillion-dollar projects (Svara 2003). Women leaders bring a unique worldview and a competitive edge that could be vital to the success of any business.

Theoretical Lens and Conceptual Framework

The conceptual framework of this study is shown in figure 1 and begins with an understanding of the masculine construction of leadership, which incorporates Schein's foundational theory of gender bias, "Think

Manager—Think Male" (1993) and Eagly & Karau's role congruity theory (2002), which describes the characteristics of agentic behavior (aggressive, determined, ambitious, and task focused) versus communal
behavior (interpersonal, empathetic, friendly, and compassionate) in
leadership. These theories of gendered stereotypes of leadership create
the organizational landscape that women must navigate in order to
reach senior leadership positions.

The second element, gender bias, often stems from the fact that
women who behave in ways that are viewed as agentic or counterstereotypical are sanctioned for violating female stereotypes of supportiveness, submissiveness, and sensitivity (Eagly & Karau 2002; Gupta
2013; Heilman, Wallen, Fuchs, & Tamkins 2004). Heilman's lack of fit
model (2001) and Rudman's status incongruity hypothesis (2012) support this view of gender disparity. Related to gender bias is one of the
most pernicious forces that women encounter: gender backlash (Garcia-
Retamero & Lopez-Zafra 2006; Heilman, Wallen, Fuchs, & Tamkins
2004; O'Neill & O'Reilly 2011). Gender backlash is the third element
of the framework. The status incongruity hypothesis (SIH) maintains
that women who violate gender-based behavior expectations will experience a negative backlash effect and be punished (Eagly & Karau 2002;
O'Neill & O'Reilly 2011; Rudman, Moss-Racusin, Phelan & Nauts 2012;
Rudman & Phelan 2008).

The fourth element of the conceptual framework draws from gender schema theories (Lemons & Parzinger 2007) and theories of gendered organizations (Acker 2006; Ridgeway 2009). Women seeking
positions of leadership in male-dominated professions often encounter
cultural "inequality regimes" (Acker 2006, 443) and report that they
do not feel as though they fit and do not belong (Wentling & Thomas
2009).

The theories that describe how women overcome gender backlash and bias provide the last element of the conceptual framework.
Self-monitoring (Gupta 2013; O'Neill & O'Reilly 2011), impression

management (Hirshfield 2011; O'Neill & O'Reilly 2011), political skill (Shaughnessy, Treadway, Breland, Williams, & Brouer 2011), and performance (Jalbert, Jalbert, & Furumo 2013) are all elements to be explored within the study. Bandura's social cognitive theory (2001) is central to the entire study as it describes the concept of self-efficacy.

Research Question

The overall research question that guided this study was:

> What are the lived experiences of women in senior leadership who have used buffering behaviors to overcome gender bias and achieve success?

Definition of Key Terms

The following terms and acronyms were used throughout the study, and the definitions provide a context for the major themes and concepts of the phenomenon under investigation.

Agentic behaviors: Agentic behaviors are typically associated with masculine behaviors of assertiveness, competitiveness, and dominance (Eagly & Wood 1991).

Buffering behaviors: Buffering behaviors are skills and strategies that utilize knowledge of self-monitoring, impression management, and political skill to overcome gender backlash against women who behave in counterstereotypical ways (Shaughnessy, Treadway, Breland, Williams, & Brouer 2011).

Communal behaviors: Communal behaviors are typically associated with feminine behaviors of friendliness, unselfishness, and compassion (Eagly & Wood 1991).

Gender schema: Gender schema are deeply embedded beliefs developed early in life regarding appropriate gender behavior, thereby making the reshaping of views of gender roles in the workplace difficult (Lemons & Parzinger 2007).

Impression management: Impression management is a conscious process by which an individual seeks to influence the perception that others will form of him or her (Hirshfield 2011; O'Neill & O'Reilly 2011).

Leaky pipeline: The leaky pipeline is a metaphor for the attrition of women in STEM as they advance in the profession (Soe & Yakura 2008).

Male hegemony: Male hegemony is defined as a pattern of practices and traits that define the criteria for the idealized man. The concept is viewed as a way to perpetuate male dominance in a particular culture (Page, Bailey, & VanDelinder 2009).

Political Skill: Political skill is "the ability to understand others at work and to use such knowledge to influence others in ways that enhance one's personal organizational objectives" (Kolodinsky, Treadway, & Ferris 2007, 1750).

Role Congruity Theory of Prejudice: The role congruity theory of prejudice is defined as the incongruency between traditionally held views of appropriate behavior for women and the characteristics believed to be required for successful leadership (Eagly & Karau 2002).

Self-efficacy: Self-efficacy is defined as "people's beliefs about their capabilities to produce levels of performance that exercise influence over events that affect their lives" (Kelsey 2007, 58).

Self-monitoring: Self-monitoring is the action of closely observing social cues and using this information to guide one's behavior (O'Neill & O'Reilly 2011).

Self-regulation: Self-regulation is the act of consciously choosing behaviors that will shape the perceptions that others form of an individual (Bandura 2001; Gupta 2013; O'Neill & O'Reilly 2011).

Status Incongruity Hypothesis (SIH): The SIH holds that when women violate feminine gender stereotypes, they often experience economic and social sanctions (Rudman 2012).

STEM: This acronym, attributed to Judith Ramaley while a director at NSF (National Science Foundation) in 2001, is widely known as the disciplines of science, technology, engineering, and mathematics (Donhoe 2013).

Assumptions and Limitations

For the purpose of this research, it was assumed that the participants have encountered some form of gender bias and backlash as they sought leadership roles in male-dominated STEM fields. The study was limited to women who have attained senior leadership positions in fields of science, technology, engineering, and mathematics. Women in other professions or at entry level or midlevel management were not included in the study and may limit the generalization of the results. Women who have not broken through the glass ceiling may hold different views and experiences from the women in the study who have achieved senior leadership status. The participants were selected based on their willingness to be interviewed and may be seen as a convenience sample, inadvertently excluding participants with differing points of view. The participants were from North American organizations, and it is acknowledged that cultural norms regarding gender differ in other parts of the world. These differences in cross-cultural gender norms may also limit the generalizability of findings to other cultural populations.

Organization of Remaining Chapters

Chapter 2 includes a review of current and foundational literature documenting the gender-based challenges, barriers, and obstacles that many women encounter as they strive to reach the upper levels of leadership. Also included is literature on the use of buffering behaviors to overcome these obstacles. The theoretical foundation and conceptual framework, both based on the tenets of social cognitive theory, will also be presented (Bandura 2001; Bussey & Bandura 1999; Chen 2006).

In chapter 3, a description of the research design and methodology used to investigate the phenomenon is outlined. Major elements contained in chapter 3 include a review of the problem and the purpose of the study, the research approach, design and paradigm, the participants, the data collection procedures, the data analysis approach, steps taken to ensure research quality, and delineations and limitations of the study. In chapter 4 of the dissertation, the results of the data collection and analysis are summarized and discussed. Chapter 5 presents the themes that emerged from the findings and offers recommendations for future research.

Summary

By exploring the meaning of women's experiences in overcoming gender bias to reach senior leadership positions, this phenomenological study provides insights into "the complexities of human life and the fullness of our experience of it" (Gibson & Hanes 2003, 182). Documenting the experiences, feelings, concerns, and reactions of women who have overcome gender bias can illuminate gender-based stereotypes, biases, and behaviors and perhaps, one day, eliminate them (Brooks & Nagy Hesse-Biber 2007). A feminist phenomenological study that describes the experience of overcoming gender bias as women strive to achieve leadership goals may provide inspiration and guidance to other women who share similar aspirations (Brooks & Nagy Hesse-Biber 2007).

Literature Review

Introduction

The purpose of this feminist phenomenological study is to discover and share women's experiences with behaviors and strategies that mitigate the effect of gender-based barriers to senior-level leadership positions in the male-dominated professions of science, technology, engineering, and mathematics (STEM).

This chapter includes both foundational and current thinking regarding the obstacles that many women encounter as they seek to advance in their careers and the mitigating mechanisms known as buffering behaviors that have lessened the impact of some of these obstacles. The goal of the chapter is to identify gaps in the literature, make additional contributions to the body of knowledge, and provide a theoretical lens for investigating the research questions. This literature review consists of seven sections: "The Theoretical Perspective"; "Beliefs and World Views of the Researcher"; "The Theoretical Framework;" "A Conceptual Overview"; "Five Conceptual Themes (Masculine Stereotypes of Leadership, Gender Bias, Gender Backlash, Gendered Organizations, and Buffering Behaviors)"; "A Synthesis of Research Findings"; and "Appropriateness of Methodology."

An extensive body of literature documents the obstacles that women encounter as they strive to reach the upper levels of leadership (Brannstrom 2004; Brooks & Hesse-Biber 2007; Eagly & Karau 2002; Garcia-Retamero & Lopez-Zafra 2006; Glick 2001; Laud & Johnson 2013; Lemons & Parzinger 2007; Page, Bailey & VanDelinder 2009; Weele & Heilman 2005). Research on experiences of women who have overcome these gendered obstacles to reach senior executive roles, particularly in male-dominated STEM fields, is lacking. Chapter 2 of this phenomenological study presents an overview of the literature regarding both the gender-based barriers that women encounter and the experiences of women who have developed mitigating mechanisms on their journey to the top of traditionally male-dominated STEM organizations. The literature review includes a discussion of the masculine stereotypes of leadership, gender bias, gender backlash, and gendered organizations. Chapter 2 also explores the mitigating strategies or buffering behaviors (Cech, Rubineau, Silbey, & Seron 2011; Gupta 2013; O'Neill & O'Reilly 2011; Shaughnessy, Treadway, Breland, Williams, & Brouer 2011; Todd, Harris, Harris, & Wheeler 2009) of self-monitoring, impression management, political skill, and performance. Social cognitive theory, which holds that people may choose how to react to environmental conditions and thereby shape outcomes, provides a foundation for understanding the potential use of buffering behaviors (Bandura 2001; Bussey & Bandura 1999; Chen 2006).

Theoretical Perspective

A theoretical perspective provides the lens through which the researcher examines and analyzes the data collected, both from the literature and from the participants. This study incorporates a feminist epistemology that informs a critical advocacy paradigm. The goal of a critical advocacy paradigm is the empowerment of individuals and the discovery of knowledge that could lead to change (Ponterotto 2005).

Critical advocacy maintains that particular social forces ignore or suppress the voices of certain populations (Ponterotto 2005). Feminist theory focuses the research on the experiences specific to women. The goal of this study is to capture and describe the lived experiences of women who have used buffering behaviors to overcome gender-based barriers to career advancement. By bringing to light leadership inequities, the exclusion of talented individuals, and the strategies that have been successful in overcoming these barriers, the author hopes that these findings will assist more women in breaking through the barriers that block their upward progress. Discovering and making known the strategies that have enabled some women to overcome gender-based barriers and hold leadership positions may empower other women in male-dominated professions to strive for similar success.

A feminist theory framework seeks to ensure that women's viewpoints, experiences, and perspectives are equally valued and reflected (Brooks & Hesse-Biber 2007; Landman 2006). This research design focuses exclusively on the views and experiences of women who have encountered discrimination and marginalization based on their gender and rose to positions of leadership in STEM organizations. Feminist research tenets seek to ensure that research (a) is focused on the social realities of women, (b) informs policies, practices, and decisions that are fair and inclusive (c) utilizes a collaborative model of inquiry between the participant and the researcher, and (d) exposes existing stereotypes and replaces them with descriptions of women's lived experiences (Landman 2006). This methodology places women at the center of the study.

The intersection of a feminist theory framework within a critical theory paradigm provides an effective approach for ensuring the points of view and lived experiences of women seeking leadership positions are included in the body of knowledge of organizational theory. These approaches question traditional ways of knowing and begin with the formulation of the research questions, continue throughout the data collection process, and culminate in the research findings. Feminist theory holds that women have insights into the social systems in which they operate because they observe and experience the worlds of both those in power and those who are not (Brooks & Hesse-Biber 2007). This study uses a critical advocacy paradigm that incorporates a feminist viewpoint to ensure that the research produced encompasses and accurately represents the social realities of women.

Theoretical Framework

This study is set within the framework of Bandura's social cognitive theory (Bandura 1994, 2001; Bandura, Caprara, Barbaranelli, Gerbino, & Pastorelli 2003; Bussey & Bandura 1999; Chen 2006), which holds that individuals can consciously learn and choose behaviors that will influence outcomes within their environments. Social cognitive theory supports the feminist research goals of fostering empowerment for women and "improving the life chances and choices for women" (Brooks & Hesse-Biber 2007, 4). Two aspects of social cognitive theory, self-regulation and self-efficacy, are central to the study. Self-regulation is defined as the ability to "perceive, evaluate and regulate behavior" and self-efficacy is described as "people's beliefs in their capabilities to produce desired effects by their own actions" (Bandura 2001, 10). This foundational theory serves as a lens through which to explore the experiences and beliefs of women leaders who have or are striving to overcome the gender-based barriers often found in traditionally male professions of STEM. Bandura's agentic perspective of social cognitive theory (2001) maintains that people "consciously and purposively access and process information to select, construct, regulate, and evaluate courses of action" (p. 12). This aspect of social cognitive theory emphasizes the importance of thoughts, perceptions, and reactions to experiences, and for this reason is appropriate for a phenomenological study.

Conceptual Overview and Definition

Chapter 2 of this study is organized conceptually around the topics, concepts, and themes for understanding the lived experiences of the women in this study who have overcome gender-based barriers and reached senior positions of leadership in male-dominated professions. The conceptual framework of this study addresses four gender-based barriers that women often encounter: the masculine stereotype of leadership, gender bias, gender backlash, and gendered organizations. The conceptual theme of buffering behaviors (self-management, impression management, political skill, and performance) may provide insights into the experiences of mitigating the negative impact of gender-based bias.

Figure 2. Conceptual framework of self-efficacious women utilizing buffering behaviors to overcome gender barriers. Self-efficacy is the essential ingredient buffering behaviors.

These constructs—gender-based barriers and buffering behaviors—form a conceptual framework that describe the challenges that many women encounter when they seek to contribute their talents, knowledge, abilities, and skills to the arena of STEM leadership (Fox & Colatrella 2006; Garcia-Retamero & Lopez-Zafra 2006; Page, Bailey, & VanDelinder 2009). This study is designed to contribute to the body of knowledge regarding the experiences of women who have utilized buffering behaviors when confronting gender bias and gender backlash and to share this knowledge with women who aspire to be leaders.

Conceptual Theme 1: Masculine Stereotypes of Leadership and Male Hegemony

Carlyle's "Great Man" theory of leadership (Borgatta, Bales, & Couch 1954) was one of the earliest examples of the view that strong leaders are associated with masculine traits and behaviors. Male stereotypes have permeated traditional views of leadership, thereby suggesting leadership to be a predominantly male domain (Borgatta et al. 1954). Early books and articles on leadership illustrate the masculine stereotype. Examples include *The Organization Man* (Whyte 1956), *The End of Economic Man,* (Drucker 1939), and *The Future of Industrial Man* (Drucker 1942). These examples of mainstream literature on the topic of leadership show that references to women were largely absent and that the "ideology, symbolism, and imagery" of leadership is most often masculine in nature (Kauaria 2002, 17; Olsson & Walker 2003).

The conceptual framework of this study begins with an understanding of the masculine construction of leadership, which incorporates Schein's foundational theory of gender bias, "Think Manager—Think Male" (1993) and Eagly and Karau's role congruity theory (2002).

In Koenig, Eagly, Mitchell, and Ristikari's (2011) landmark study "Are Leader Stereotypes Masculine? A Meta-analysis of Three Research Paradigms," the authors posed the research question, "How strong is the evidence for the masculinity of leader stereotypes?" (p. 617). The sixty-nine studies in the meta-analysis found that the cultural stereotypes of leaders continue to be masculine (Koenig, Eagly, Mitchell, & Ristikari 2011). The meta-analysis included three gender-based research paradigms: Schein's think manager—think male paradigm, Powell and Butterfield's agency-communion paradigm, and Schein's masculinity-femininity paradigm (as cited in Koenig et al. 2011). The goal of the meta-analysis was to determine the presence of masculinity in leader stereotypes. In her conclusion, Koenig stated, "All three paradigms showed that stereotypes of leaders are decidedly masculine ... people viewed leaders as quite similar to men but not very similar to women, as more agentic than communal, and as more masculine than feminine" (Koenig et al. 2011, 634). The fact that the workforce was predominantly male when these theories were being examined must be taken into account. The concern is that these views of leadership being a masculine trait have persisted into the present (Schein & Davidson 1993; Smith 2010).

Authors of a fifteen-year follow-up study of Schein's research found that the gender stereotypes of the think manager—think male paradigm persist among many male business management students, and their views remain similar to the majority of male managers of the 1970s (Schein & Davidson 1993; Smith 2010). In both studies, however, researchers examined paradigms that are over fifteen years old. Recent studies have shown that stereotypical beliefs about male and female gender roles change when an individual is repeatedly exposed to counterstereotypical examples, experiences, and information (Paris & Decker 2012). Leadership stereotypes are beginning to change, and certain feminine leadership styles have been rated as more effective under specified conditions (Madden 2011).

Another important aspect for consideration when examining the masculine stereotype of leadership is the concept of masculine hegemony, or "the maintenance of practices that allowed men's dominance over women to continue" (Connell & Messerschmidt 2005, 832). Of particular interest in this area of masculinity research is that those who belong to the hegemonic group (in this case males), generally do not question the culture and policies that maintain hegemony (Page, Bailey, & VanDelinder 2009; Sheridan & Milgate 2003). Male hegemony provides a construct within which to examine the experiences of women as they seek to achieve positions of senior leadership in science, technology, engineering, and mathematics (STEM) (Page, Bailey, & VanDelinder 2009).

An alternative view of the masculine stereotype of leadership as a barrier to aspiring women was presented in a study that found "women were less likely than men to desire promotion into a senior management position" (Litzky & Greenhaus 2007, 637). Other studies presenting different positions on masculine stereotypes of leadership report that women actually have a gendered advantage because women are generally believed to be better equipped to respond to contemporary leadership requirements by utilizing the feminine leadership attributes (Evans 2010). These attributes include a high degree of emotional and cultural intelligence, an ability to empower others and to share leadership, a focus on customer service and employee welfare, and a more considerate and caring leadership style (Evans 2010).

There are women who have found ways to successfully overcome traditional beliefs of the masculine construct of leadership and attain senior executive positions. It is important that researchers study both the barriers to aspiring women and the experiences of women who have been effective in overcoming these barriers. Bandura's social cognitive theory posits that people are agentic, capable of acting with intentionality to produce outcomes and "to originate actions for given purposes" (Bandura 2001, 6). This study provides insights into the lives of women who have experienced the use of agentic, self-directed behaviors when encountering masculine stereotypes of leadership.

Conceptual Theme 2: Gender Bias

As shown in figure 3, the second element of the study's conceptual framework explores the concept of gender bias, which leads to the unequal treatment of women as they compete in male-dominated professions (Brooks & Hesse-Biber 2007; Eagly & Karau 2002; Glick & Fiske 2001; Heilman 2001; Weele & Heilman 2005). A preliminary review of the literature finds that as women attempt to achieve senior leadership positions, they often encounter obstacles and challenges, both benign and hostile, to their upward career progress that appear to be specifically related to gender bias (Brannstrom 2004; Eagly & Karau 2002; Glick 2001; Glick & Fiske 2001; Laud & Johnson 2013; Weele & Heilman 2005). The ProQuest search tool available through the Chicago School of Professional Psychology yielded 32,230 results based on the search terms *gender bias*. A search for *bias* in STEM professions produced 2,341 peer reviewed journal articles and/or dissertations. The preponderance of research on gender bias indicates that this issue continues to generate discussion and controversy.

There are two forms of gender bias, hostile and benign. Hostile gender bias is the antipathy directed toward women who seek positions of power that men traditionally hold (Glick & Fiske 2001). Benign gender bias is a benevolent, chivalrous, protective attitude toward women who adopt conventional roles (Glick & Fiske 2001). Gender bias is often subtle and deniable, and unless data are presented in aggregate form, organizations will ignore it (Crosby, Clayton, Alksnis, & Hemker 1986). Heilman's lack of fit model (2001) and Rudman's status incongruity hypothesis (2012) address gender bias by providing evidence of prevalent gendered beliefs regarding the different social and organizational roles of men and of women.

In Luster's (2011) phenomenological study of women who rose to senior executive positions, all nine of the participants reported facing both direct and indirect gender discrimination and bias. These findings supported the feminist view that attitudes toward women often negatively affect career advancement opportunities (Luster 2011). In studies on formal and informal forms of gender bias and discrimination, Weele and Heilman (2005) found that many of the obstacles that women encountered were subtle and intangible. These included "an inhospitable corporate culture" (p. 31) that excludes women from informal networks of communication. This same study found that men were significantly less likely than women are to believe these factors of bias were present or inhibited advancement (Weele & Heilman 2005).

A powerful barrier that women frequently encounter based on gender bias is that of entrenched beliefs regarding the inability of women to handle certain jobs (Barsh & Yee 2011). This perceived disparity between feminine gender roles and masculine leadership roles results in two forms of bias: (1) women are generally seen as less likely to be successful in leadership positions and (2) when women do behave in stereotypically masculine leadership styles, they are often viewed unfavorably (Eagly & Karau 2002).

In a global study of gender-based perceptions of leadership, Sikdar and Mitra (2009) found that gender bias is present when determining the characteristics needed to be a successful leader. Desirable masculine behaviors were characterized as "aggressive, risk-taking, decisive, and autonomous" while desirable feminine behaviors were characterized as "kind, caring, relational, and humble" (Sikdar & Mitra 2009, 2). These characteristics appeared to create deep-seated beliefs and expectations of appropriate or authentic leadership behaviors (Sikdar & Mitra 2009). This creates another challenge for many aspiring women as they navigate organizational cultures.

The role congruity theory of prejudice (Eagly & Karau 2002) holds that women who seek leadership roles will experience bias because of the incongruency between traditionally held views of appropriate behavior for women and the characteristics believed to be required for successful leadership. When descriptive norms (what members of a group are perceived to typically do), and injunctive norms (what members of a class are ideally expected to do) come into conflict, those who are behaving incongruently will commonly experience gender prejudice (Eagly & Karau 2002).

A similar view is found in Heilman's (1983, 1997) lack of fit model in which "the perceived lack of fit between the requirements of traditionally male jobs and the stereotypic attributes ascribed to women is likely to produce expectations of failure" (p. 660). The perceived incongruity between female gender stereotypes and leadership stereotypes, which are typically male, is another factor that can result in gender bias (Heilman, Wallen, Fuchs, & Tamkins 2004). People generally report that they respect and admire leaders who demonstrate authenticity (Smith 2010). However, ingrained gender stereotypes lead many people to judge men who are behaving in an agentic way as authentic, but when women behave in agentic ways, they are often seen as contradicting stereotypical norms of female behavior and viewed as inauthentic (Smith 2010).

Gender schema concepts suggest another source of potential gender bias (Lemons & Parzinger 2007). Gender schemas are beliefs regarding appropriate gender behavior often resulting from the social practices of the culture in which one grows up (Lemons & Parzinger 2007). Gender schemas develop early in life, are deeply embedded, and make the reshaping of views of gender roles in the workplace daunting (Lemons & Parzinger 2007). Another significant barrier that women often encounter and need to overcome will be gender schemas that appear to be deeply entrenched and ingrained (Lemons & Parzinger 2007).

Conceptual Theme 3: Gender Backlash

The third conceptual element of the study encompasses a problematic double bind that aspiring women often face, known as gender backlash (Garcia-Retamero & Lopez-Zafra 2006; Heilman, Wallen, Fuchs, & Tamkins 2004; O'Neill & O'Reilly 2011). Rudman and Fairchild (2004) introduced the concept of gender backlash and defined it as "social and economic sanctions for counter-stereotypical behavior" (Rudman & Fairchild 2004, 157; Rudman, Moss-Racusin, Phelan, & Nauts 2012, 166). Extensive research on gender backlash has also shown that when women incorporate behaviors that are considered masculine such as self-promotion, hard negotiating, competiveness, or assertiveness they are frequently viewed negatively and not selected for senior leadership roles (Glick 2001; Gupta 2013; Heilman, Wallen, Fuchs, & Tamkins 2004; Moss-Racusin & Rudman 2010; O'Neill & O'Reilly 2011; Rudman, Moss-Racusin, Phelan, & Nauts 2012; Rudman & Phelan 2008). The status incongruity hypothesis (SIH) maintains that when women violate feminine gender stereotypes they will often experience backlash through economic and social sanctions (Eagly & Karau 2002; O'Neill & O'Reilly 2011; Rudman, Moss-Racusin, Phelan, & Nauts 2012; Rudman & Phelan 2008). It appears that gender backlash discourages some women from seeking leadership positions and serves to perpetuate the dominance of male leadership in organizations (Rudman & Fairchild 2004).

Studies show that women holding leadership positions must demonstrate stereotypically masculine behaviors of aggressiveness, dominance, and toughness (Weele & Heilman 2005). However, Glick's study (2001) on gender stereotypes showed that peers, subordinates, and supervisors rate women who do exhibit stereotypically male behaviors as **"having interpersonal skills problems and/or being unlikable"** (p. 113). The traditional role perceptions of leadership as a predominantly masculine domain can lead to a double bind of role incongruity and can result in subsequent backlash directed toward women who behave incongruently and counterstereotypically (Moss-Racusin & Rudman 2010; O'Neill & O'Reilly 2011). As shown in figure 3, gender backlash is another obstacle that women who seek leadership positions in male-dominated fields must overcome.

In a comprehensive analysis of five studies on gender backlash, Rudman, Moss-Racusin, Phelan, and Nauts (2012) posed the research question "what is it about competent, ambitious women that put them at risk for social rejection and backlash behaviors?" (p. 166). The primary purpose of the study was to determine what motivates backlash. The findings of the five studies in Rudman et al. (2012) supported the double bind phenomenon women often report that results from the perception that women's gender status is lower than men's, so they must utilize agentic behaviors (e.g., career-oriented, assertive, independent, ambitious, self-starter, high self-esteem, and competitive) to be viewed as qualified for leadership (Rudman et al. 2012). However, women who violate gender norms and behave in a gender inappropriate fashion frequently face sanctions and penalties. The penalties are often in the form of exclusion from consideration for senior leadership roles and relegation to secondary nonleadership positions (Garcia-Retamero & Lopez-Zafra 2006; Oakley 2000; Page, Bailey, & VanDelinder 2009).

Additional findings of the Rudman et al. (2012) study indicated that women who behaved agentically experienced sabotage more often than any other group. However, women in leadership who used extreme diplomacy were able to avoid backlash behaviors. The researchers concluded that it was not a woman's senior position that provoked backlash, but a woman's agentic behavior that did (Rudman et al. 2012). A similar study showed that niceness was a quality expected of women, and when they behaved authoritatively or aggressively, they would frequently encounter backlash responses (Babcock & Laschever 2003).

A related study showed that those who occupied gender incongruent positions of leadership faced higher standards of performance and more severe penalties for mistakes (Brescoll, Dawson, & Uhlmann 2010). Gender devaluation is a subtle form of gender bias (i.e., if a woman holds a senior leadership position, the position loses value) (Monroe, Ozyurt, Wrigley, & Alexander 2008).

Conceptual Theme 4: Gendered Organizations and Cultures

The fourth element of the conceptual framework draws from the theories of gendered organizations and cultures, often found in male-dominated professions, in this case STEM. Gender schema theories (Cech, Rubineau, Silbey, & Seron 2011; Lemons & Parzinger 2007) and theories of gendered organizations (Skinner 2006) inform this conceptual element of the research design.

Acker (2006) argued that organizations that grant power to some and not to others based on class, gender, and race create "inequality regimes" (Acker 2006, 443). Many women in organizations with inequality regimes report that the culture of their organization leaves them feeling they are "outsiders who do not belong" (Acker 2006, 446). Descriptions of STEM organizations and cultures include phrases such as "largely white, male dominated, anti-social, individualistic, and competitive" (Wentling & Thomas 2009, 27). As a result, women often perceive the STEM culture as one in which they would not fit (Wentling & Thomas 2009). In a study of workplace cultures, female participants from STEM organizations identified those organizational cultural characteristics that most impeded their upward mobility (Wentling & Thomas 2009). The most frequently named cultural characteristic impeding women's career progress was the "male dominated, good old boy" nature of the culture (Wentling & Thomas 2009, 31). The next highest ranked cultural characteristic that proved negative for women was "a very competitive culture" (Wentling & Thomas 2009, 31). The third ranked cultural characteristic that women found exclusionary was "diversity not valued" (Wentling & Thomas 2009, 31). The fourth and fifth ranked characteristics were the "very conservative" nature of the company and the "lack of consensus seeking" (Wentling & Thomas 2009, 31). The last two of the seven characteristics were elements of "exclusivity" described as being made to feel like an outsider and "a hostile environment" (Wentling & Thomas 2009, 31).

Heilman's lack of fit model has been linked to a perceived lack of fit with an organizational culture (Lyness & Thompson 2000). In a study of sixty-nine female executives and sixty-nine male executives, more women reported lack of organizational fit as a greater barrier to career advancement than did men (Lyness & Thompson 2000). Individuals often base decisions to join or leave an organization on psychological factors including "attitudes, organizational climate, and leadership" (Schneider 1987, 439). In traditionally male organizations, the cultural climate has often been reported as inhospitable to women and may be a factor in women's attrition (Acker 2006; Fox & Colatrella 2006; Lemons & Parzinger 2001; Von Hellens, Nielsen, & Trauth 2001; Wentling & Thomas 2009). Women working in STEM occupations and organizations frequently report these cultures as highly gendered (Acker 2006; Fox & Colatrella 2006; Lemons & Parzinger 2001; Wentling & Thomas 2009). Other researchers have maintained that women's absence from leadership in STEM organizations is not a result of gender-based barriers, but is instead a result of women's choices regarding motherhood and child rearing (Ceci & Williams 2011). This alternative view of the underrepresentation of women in STEM leadership holds that a woman's decision to have children affects her ability to have a demanding research career with irregular hours and that gendered organizations are not the cause of the scarcity of women (Ceci & Williams 2011).

Conceptual Theme 5: Buffering Behaviors

The first four elements of the conceptual framework describe the organizational challenges confronting many women and include (a) the generally held belief that leadership is a masculine domain, (b) the gender stereotypes that lead to bias, (c) gender backlash when women behave counterstereotypically, and (d) the gendered nature of many STEM organizations. Yet, there are women who persist, persevere, and succeed in reaching senior levels of leadership in STEM professions. What are the life experiences, strategies, beliefs, and behaviors that enable certain women to overcome the gender-based barriers to their upward progression? It is important to understand the experience of women who have surmounted the obstacles that prevented many talented, experienced, and qualified women from entering the executive suite in representative numbers. The last element of the conceptual framework examines buffering behaviors and the role they may play in the lives of women who have overcome gender-based barriers and challenges.

Central to Bandura's social cognitive theory (2001) is self-efficacy, an individual's conviction that through his or her choices, actions, and strategies, obstacles can be overcome, difficulties can be resolved, and goals can be attained (Bandura 2001). Self-efficacy encompasses "people's beliefs about their capabilities to produce designated levels of performance that exercise influence over events that affect their lives (Bandura 1994, 71). An individual's level of self-efficacy determines his or her likelihood to enter into challenging situations, to persist in the face of setbacks, and to find ways to achieve desired outcomes (Bandura 2001).

Recent studies have shown that certain buffering behaviors enable many self-efficacious women to overcome the gender-based challenges they often encounter as they seek to attain senior leadership roles in STEM organizations (Cech, Rubineau, Silbey, & Seron 2011; Gupta 2013; Jalbert, Jalbert, & Furumo 2013; O'Neill & O'Reilly 2011; Shaughnessy et al. 2011; Todd, Harris, Harris, & Wheeler 2009). Figure 4 illustrates the buffering behaviors, which have often proven to be effective in many women's success in achieving senior leadership positions in traditionally male-dominated professions. These buffering behaviors include, but are not limited to, self-monitoring (Bandura 2001; Gupta 2013; O'Neill & O'Reilly 2011) impression management (Hirshfield 2011; O'Neill & O'Reilly 2011; Singh, Kumra, & Vinnicombe 2002), political skill (Shaughnessy, Treadway, Breland, Williams, & Brouer 2011; Todd, Harris, Harris, & Wheeler 2009), and performance (Jalbert, Jalbert, & Furumo 2013). Self-efficacy is the foundation of buffering behaviors because it influences "cognitive, motivational, decisional, and affective determinants" (Bandura, Caprara, Barbaranelli, Gerbino, & Pastorelli 2003, 769).

An appropriate area in which to examine the experiences of women with buffering behaviors would be the lives of women scientists, technologists, engineers, and mathematicians who reached the senior executive level in their organizations. This study presents the findings of that inquiry.

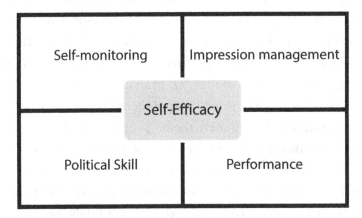

Figure 3. The buffering behaviors of self-monitoring, impression management, political skill, and performance all utilize some degree of self-efficacy and are effective in overcoming gender-based barriers to advancement

Self-monitoring as a buffering behavior. Self-monitoring is a behavioral technique in which people assess and adjust their behavior within interpersonal and organizational situations and appears to be an effective buffering strategy for overcoming gender bias and backlash (Flynn & Ames 2006; Rudman & Phelan 2008; Shivers-Blackwell 2006). People who self-monitor closely observe social cues and use this information to guide their behavior, which is particularly helpful to women in organizations where strong gender norms exist (O'Neill & O'Reilly 2011). Studies have shown that self-monitoring has a positive effect on promotions, interview success, and performance ratings (Flynn & Ames 2006; O'Neill & O'Reilly 2011). Studies have also shown that self-monitoring is effective in overcoming negative gender stereotypes (Flynn & Ames 2006). In studies of work groups consisting of both men and women, women who were high self-monitors were rated as more influential and more likely to emerge as leaders in the group than men and women who were low self-monitors (Shivers-Blackwell 2006).

Impression management as a buffering behavior. Impression management, also known as self-presentation, is a conscious process by which individuals seek to create a specific impression on others to elicit certain reactions (Guadagno & Cialdini 2007; Singh, Kumra, & Vinnicombe 2002). Goffman (1959) introduced the concept of impression management and observed that "it is in an individual's best interests to influence other people's perceptions of themselves in order to control others' conduct and reactions to them" (p. 6) He noted that one's choice of actions could influence the outcomes of a situation (Goffman 1959). Before an individual can successfully utilize impression management techniques, he or she must know what behaviors the other person will view positively or negatively and behave accordingly (Goffman 1959). Women in STEM professions are often viewed as less expert than their male counterparts (Singh, Kumra, & Vinnicombe 2002) and the impression management technique of self-promotion has been used effectively to counteract those perceptions (Gilrane 2013). Gardner and Martinko (1988) linked Goffman's impression management (IM) theory (1959) to organizational theory and posited, "IM behaviors are potentially related to individual success and promotability within organizations" (p. 321).

Political skill as a buffering behavior. Organizations are political in nature, and career advancement is frequently associated with politically astute behavior (Mintzberg 1985). Politically effective behavior is defined as "the ability to effectively understand others at work and to use such knowledge to influence others to act in ways that enhance one's personal and/or organizational objectives" (Ferris, Treadway, Kolodinsky, Hochwarter, Kacmar, Douglas, & Frink 2005, 127). Studies examining the relationship between political skill and individual career outcomes found that politically skillful people had higher promotability ratings (Gentry, Gilmore, Shuffler, & Leslie 2012; Kolodinsky, Treadway, & Ferris 2007). Political skill enables many women to overcome gender-based barriers to their career advancement (Gentry, Gilmore, Shuffler, & Leslie 2012; Shaughnessy et al. 2011). Further, politically skilled women who employ buffering mechanisms can engage in counterstereotypical behavior without eliciting a backlash response (Shaughnessy et al. 2011). Highly achieving women that exhibit extreme diplomacy are generally able to avoid backlash (Rudman et al. 2012). In a recent study, the use of political skill led to a reduction in the backlash often experienced when a woman deviates from traditional gender roles (Shaughnessy et al. 2011). Supervisors frequently like politically skillful women better and have rated them more highly on assessments of advancement potential (Shaughnessy et al. 2011). Research indicates that women with high levels of political skill were more likely to achieve leadership positions when working in male-dominated organizations (Marla & Smith 2014; Shaughnessy et al. 2011).

Performance as a buffering behavior. Global competition in science and technology is growing rapidly and many STEM companies are struggling to remain financially viable in these innovation-driven markets. The National Council of Women in Technology offers compelling evidence that when diverse people with different points of view work together to design IT solutions, the solutions are more effective and widely accepted (Rose & Thomas 2009). A recent summary of multiple studies on gender-diverse teams in IT reveals that these teams "demonstrate superior productivity and financial performance compared with homogenous teams" (Barker, Mancha, & Ashcraft 2014, 2). Similarly, research in organizations ranging from manufacturing to science and engineering indicate that women often outperform their male colleagues on measures of financial performance, leadership, and management ability (Reinhold 2005). Peers, bosses, and subordinates rated female executives higher than male executives on measures of producing high-quality work, setting goals, and mentoring (Reinhold 2005).

Increasingly, organizations are recognizing that gender diverse leadership teams produce stronger business results than male-only teams (Barsh & Yee 2011; Herring 2009; Jalbert, Jalbert, & Furumo 2013; Watson, Kumar, & Michaelsen 1993). Many organizations are abandoning the good old boys network approach to filling leadership slots and are using proven business performance criteria to select leaders (Barker, Mancha, & Ashcraft 2014; Barsh & Yee 2011; Dezsö & Ross 2012). Ample evidence exists to support the business case for gender equity in leadership and that gender diversity positively affects financial performance (Barker, Mancha, & Ashcraft 2014; Herring 2009; Jalbert, Jalbert, & Furumo 2013; Schipani, Dworkin, Kwolek-Folland, & Maurer 2009). A study of US based companies showed that the organizations with the highest levels of gender diversity also had higher sales revenues, customers, and market share (Herring 2009).

A study of the stock performance of twenty-six publicly traded companies headed by women found that they outperformed both the market and comparable companies headed by male CEOs (Adler 2001). A nineteen-year longitudinal study of 215 Fortune 500 companies showed that the companies with the highest percentage of women in senior leadership realized higher profits than competitors in their industry (Adler 2001). The results of a multiple regression analyses found that companies headed by female CEOs produced higher sales growth, institutional ownership, and return on investment than those headed by male CEOs (Jalbert, Jalbert, & Furumo 2013).

The lived experiences of women who have overcome gender bias and achieved leadership positions through proven performance provide successful strategies for other women in male-dominated fields (Brooks & Nagy Hesse-Biber 2007).

Synthesis of Literature Review

This literature review synthesizes the scholarly findings related to the traditional challenges that many women face as they seek roles of senior leadership. These challenges include the masculinity of leader stereo-types, gender bias, gender backlash, and gendered organizations. The conceptual framework that informs these gender-based obstacles and provides the theoretical background for framing interview questions includes Eagly and Karau's role congruity theory of prejudice (2002), Heilman's lack of fit model (1983, 1997), Rudman and Fairchild's concept of gender backlash (2004, 2012), and Acker's (2006) inequality regimes.

While the research on the gender-based barriers confronting women is extensive, much less is known about the experience of us-ing mitigating behaviors that enable some women to overcome these obstacles and achieve and maintain roles of senior leadership. These strategies, known as buffering behaviors, are beginning to be acknowl-edged generally but have not been studied specifically for women in the STEM professions organizations (Cech, Rubineau, Silbey, & Seron 2011; Gupta 2013; O'Neill & O'Reilly 2011; Shaughnessy et al. 2011; Todd, Harris, Harris, & Wheeler 2009). Buffering behaviors include political skill (Ferris, Treadway, Kolodinsky, Hochwarter, Kacmar, Douglas, & Frink 2005; Gentry, Gilmore, Shuffler, & Leslie 2012; Marla & Smith 2014; Shaughnessy, Treadway, Breland, Williams, & Brouer 2011), self-monitoring (Flynn & Ames 2006; O'Neill & O'Reilly 2011; Rudman & Phelan 2008; Shivers-Blackwell 2006) impression manage-ment (Guadagno & Cialdini 2007; Hirshfield 2011; O'Neill & O'Reilly 2011; Singh, Kumra, & Vinnicombe 2002), and performance (Adler 2009; Barker, Mancha, & Ashcraft 2014; Barsh & Yee 2011; Dezsö & Ross 2012; Jalbert, Jalbert, & Furumo 2013).

Summary

Bandura's social cognitive theory (2001) suggests that self-efficacy may be central to the ability of some women to successfully enter challeng-ing situations, be persistent, and achieve long-held goals. Self-efficacy is the foundation of these self-management buffering behaviors because it influences "cognitive, motivational, decisional, and affective determinants" (Bandura, Caprara, Barbaranelli, Gerbino, & Pastorelli 2003, 769). Women who seek positions of leadership in the male-dominated STEM professions frequently face numerous gender-based barriers and backlash. There are, however, women who have surmounted these obstacles and found ways to solve for X in a Y domain. There is a gap in the literature regarding the experience of buffering techniques of women who have overcome gender-based barriers to reach positions of leadership in STEM organizations. This study adds to the body of knowledge in this area. The lived experiences of self-efficacious women using buffering behaviors provides successful strategies for other women striving to achieve senior leadership positions in male-dominated fields and will hopefully lead to needed social and organizational change (Brooks & Hesse-Biber 2007).

The foregoing literature review presents a framework for examining the gender-based barriers that women often encounter as they seek leadership positions. Also presented is literature addressing the recent discovery of certain buffering behaviors used to mitigate these challenges. Chapter 3, "Methodology," includes a review of the research problem, the research approach, and the research design. The section on the research design addresses the methods related to the participants, sampling procedures, data collection, and data analysis. The two final sections of chapter 3 demonstrate how the methodology will ensure research quality and ethical consideration of the study. Chapter 4 presents the results of the study and identifies the themes that emerged from the data. Chapter 5 provides a structural synthesis of the themes and conclusions drawn from the findings, a discussion of the potential application of the findings, and offers suggestions for future research.

Methodology

Background

As qualified women attempt to climb the corporate ladder and reach high-level leadership positions, persistent forces block their ascent (Berry & Franks 2010; Brescoll, Dawson, & Uhlmann 2010; Reinhold 2005; Rose & Thomas 2009). Qualified women still do not hold senior executive positions in the same relative proportion as men, nor do the percentages of women in leadership positions reflect the significant number of women at midlevel management. Female leaders in the traditionally male professions of science, technology, engineering, and mathematics (STEM) are particularly scarce, and their route to senior leadership is even more arduous (Catalyst 2013; Fox & Colatrella 2006; Hewlett, Buck Luce, Servon, Sherbin, Shiller, & Sumberg 2008; Wentling & Thomas 2007).

Despite the history of gender disparity in corporate practices of leadership selection, many women have persevered and attained positions of senior leadership in the male-dominated fields of science, technology, engineering, and mathematics (STEM). The CEOs of General Motors, Hewlett Packard, IBM, and Lockheed Martin are women as are the presidents of Harvard University, Brown University, Rensselaer

Polytechnic Institute, and the University of Pennsylvania (Catalyst 2014). Studies show that women must demonstrate stereotypically masculine behaviors of aggressiveness, dominance, and toughness in order to be perceived as potential leaders (Weele & Heilman 2005). Studies on gender stereotypes showed that when women do exhibit stereotypically male behaviors, they are often rated as "having interpersonal skill problems and/or being unlikeable" (Rudman & Glick 1999, 1005). Extensive research on gender backlash has also shown that when women incorporate behaviors that are considered masculine such as self-promotion, hard negotiating, competiveness, or assertiveness they are frequently not hired, not promoted, and not liked (Glick 2001; Gupta 2013; Heilman, Wallen, Fuchs, & Tamkins 2004; Moss-Racusin & Rudman 2010; O'Neill & O'Reilly 2011; Rudman, Moss-Racusin, Phelan, & Nauts 2012; Rudman & Phelan 2008).

The status incongruity hypothesis explains this phenomenon and has shown that when women violate cultural norms regarding gender roles, they will experience prejudice and backlash (Eagly and Karau 2002; Rudman & Glick 2001; Rudman, Moss-Racusin, Phelan, & Sanne Nauts 2012). How, then, do some women overcome this double bind of gendered expectations and sanctions? What are the elements of the experience of resiliency of women who are the numerical minority in senior leadership (Richman, vanDellen, & Wood 2011)? A great deal of research has been conducted on the topic of gender inequities in leadership, but the experiences of women who succeed despite discriminatory practices as they navigate the corporate corridors to senior leadership have not been explored as thoroughly.

Researchers have recently begun to focus on certain buffering behaviors that allow women to utilize counterstereotypical agentic behavior without experiencing a gender-based backlash response (Cech, Rubineau, Silbey, & Seron 2011; Hirshfield 2011; Hopkins, O'Neil, & Bilimoria 2006; Kelsey 2007; O'Neill & O'Reilly 2011; Shaughnessy, Treadway, Breland, Williams, & Brouer 2011). The goal of this phenomenological study is to explore the essence and meaning of the lived experiences of senior female leaders who have utilized buffering behaviors as they achieved positions of leadership in the traditionally male-dominated fields of science, technology, engineering, or mathematics. The study will contribute to the body of knowledge needed to address this problem by gaining insight and understanding into the phenomenon of buffering behaviors and career advancement in male-dominated fields and by sharing these insights and skills with other aspiring women. Chapter 3 reviews the problem and purpose of the study, describes the research approach and paradigm, outlines the research design including a discussion of the participant recruitment process, the procedures for sampling, data collection, and data analysis. Additionally the chapter addresses issues related to ensuring research quality and ethical considerations.

Statement of the Problem

There is a problem in corporate organizations, government, and society related to the underrepresentation of women in senior leadership ranks, particularly in the fields of science, technology, engineering, and mathematics (STEM). This problem affects both organizations and people because it limits access to a broad array of insights, experiences, and knowledge at the senior level where leaders are making strategic decisions and formulating corporate direction. Global competition, especially in science and technology, is rapidly growing and corporate entities are under increasing pressure to produce innovative solutions and financial results (Hewlett et al. 2008).

Women in STEM report a number of obstacles to leadership including limited opportunities for professional development, exclusion from male-dominated career networks, and gender discrimination (Steinke 2013). Despite the fact that many women possess the skill, talent, and experience to be successful leaders, and it has been proven that they contribute to organizational success, their upward progress is frequently blocked (Hewlett et al. 2008; Wentling & Thomas 2007). The general problem is that despite the fact that many women possess the skill, knowledge, and expertise to be successful leaders (Barker, Mancha, & Ashcraft 2014; Barsh & Yee 2011; Evans 2010; Hopkins, O'Neil, & Bilimoria 2006) innovative problem solvers (Feyerherm & Vick 2005; Horwitz & Horwitz 2007; Rose & Thomas 2009) and exceptional contributors to the bottom line (Jalbert, Jalbert, & Furumo 2013; Welbourne, Cycyota, & Ferrante 2007), they continue to encounter barriers to upward their mobility, many of which are gender-based (Chen, Roy, & Crawford 2010; Hewlett et al. 2008; Pai & Vaidya 2009).

Recent studies have shown that there are behaviors and approaches that may attenuate backlash reactions against women who exhibit counterstereotypical behavior (Gupta 2013; Moss-Racusin & Rudman 2010; O'Neill & O'Reilly 2011; Shaughnessy, Treadway, Breland, Williams, & Brouer 2011). These mitigating behaviors are referred to as buffering behaviors and include, but are not limited to, self-monitoring (Gupta 2013; O'Neill & O'Reilly 2011), impression management (Hirshfield 2011; O'Neill & O'Reilly 2011), political skill (Shaughnessy, Treadway, Breland, Williams, & Brouer 2011), and performance (Jalbert, Jalbert, & Furumo 2013; Welbourne, Cycyota, & Ferrante 2007).

This study will add a new dimension to the body of knowledge by providing accounts of the lived experiences of women who have used buffering strategies and behaviors to overcome gender bias and backlash and to reach senior leadership positions in the STEM professions. Understanding the essence of the lived experiences of women who have overcome gender bias could provide insights for other women striving to achieve senior leadership positions in male-dominated fields and lead to needed social change (Brooks & Nagy Hesse-Biber 2007).

This study fills a gap in the literature by shifting the focus from external factors of gender discrimination to the experiences of women who have overcome the barriers found in educational systems and organizational cultures and attained senior levels of leadership (Bowles 2012; Moss-Racusin & Rudman 2010; O'Neill & O'Reilly 2011; Shaughnessy, Treadway, Breland, Williams, & Brouer 2011). **The study also shifts the focus from seeking causes of the problem and remedies to studying the solutions discovered through the actions of those who have solved the problem for themselves.**

Purpose of the Study

The specific purpose of this critical advocacy theory, feminist phenomenological study was to understand the role that buffering behaviors played in the lived experiences of women who overcame gender-based barriers and became leaders in the male-dominated fields of science, technology, engineering, and mathematics (STEM). The goal was to provide insight and understanding into the experiences of women who overcame gender discrimination and broke through the glass ceiling. Buffering behaviors are defined as the skills and strategies that utilize knowledge of self-monitoring, political behavior, impression management, and performance to overcome the gender bias and backlash women who behave in counter stereotypical ways often experience.

Research Approach/Paradigm

The researcher's ontological or philosophical beliefs about what constitute truth and her epistemological position on what constitutes knowledge creates the foundation for this study's design and methodology (Creswell 2013; Guba 1990; Marsh & Furlong 2010). Paradigms reflect the beliefs and values of the researcher (Guba 1990). This study has as its foundation a social constructivist, feminist perspective and utilizes a phenomenological strategy of inquiry. Phenomenologists seek meanings, insights, and understandings rather than explanations or cause and effect outcomes (Moustakas 1994). The social constructivist approach holds that that there are many truths and that one subjectively defines and constructs his or her concept of reality based on lived experiences (Ponterotto 2005). The individual defines and determines the meaning of an experience based on his or her interactions. In this paradigm, one person's meaning of reality is as true for him or her as another's meaning of reality is for that individual (Marsh & Furlong 2010). As such, the constructivist paradigm is a foundational element of this qualitative research study.

From a constructivist standpoint, one constructs truth and reality through social interactions with the environment, and the researcher can capture these realities through interactive dialogue and inquiry (Ponterotto 2005). This paradigm honors and gives voice to the participant's subjective impressions and interpretations of a phenomenon (Guba 1990). The social constructivist approach sees the researcher and participant as interdependent, and reality is discovered in a process of joint discovery by the "inquirer and the inquired" (Guba & Lincoln 1994, 107). Constructivists believe that there are many equally valid realities and that each individual constructs these realities based on his or her unique experience.

This study also incorporates a critical advocacy theory paradigm, which is ideological in nature and encompasses feminism (Guba 1990; Martin 2002). Critical advocacy theory maintains that society has ignored or suppressed the voices of certain populations. The feminist emphasis of this study seeks to capture the voices of women who have experienced and overcome the disparity of power based on gender. A feminist theory framework gives voice to women who have not been heard and who have been perceived to be marginalized (Lewis 2009). The aim of feminist research is to end the marginalization of women that has historically taken place in social science research (Landman 2006). Feminist theory originated, in part, to challenge the underrepresentation of women's experiences within the positivist research paradigm and to ensure that women's viewpoints, experiences, and perspectives are valued and reported (Landman 2006). This phenomenological study focused on the stories and experiences of women who encountered discrimination and marginalization based on their gender. Feminist scholars have shown that bringing together phenomenology and feminist theory is a valuable approach "for addressing the lived experiences of marginalization, invisibility, and nonnormativity" (Zeiler & Käll, eds. 2014, 1). Feminists are increasingly linking phenomenology and feminist inquiry. Fisher observed, "phenomenology shares with feminist interpretation a commitment to grounding theory in lived experience, and in revealing the way in which the world is produced through the constituting acts of subjective experience" (2000, 27). Levesque-Lopman (2000) noted that feminist phenomenology has "extraordinary potential for researching women's experiences" (p. 103). Feminist methodologies are not limited to any single mode of inquiry but have as a goal supporting research that is of value to women, acknowledges the validity of women's experiences, and advocates for social changes that advance the status of women (DeVault 1996).

These paradigms are the foundation of this qualitative phenomenological study and provide a way to understand a phenomenon through the subjective personal experiences of women who have overcome gender bias and backlash with buffering behaviors. Qualitative research is a process of open-minded discovery, one in which the researcher does not approach the study with a hypothesis to prove or disprove. A qualitative researcher approaches his or her area of interest seeking to understand why something is the way it is. The research takes place in the natural setting of the participants through in-depth interviews with words, rather than numbers, as data for analysis (Patton & Cochran 2002).

Phenomenological Methodology

The goal of a phenomenological study is to comprehend the common meaning or the essence of a phenomenon through the lived experiences of individuals who have lived in and through the experience (Moustakas 1994; Seidman 2013). This study explored women's experiences with the use of buffering behaviors to overcome gender bias. The goal of a phenomenological study is to examine a phenomenon and define truth within the framework of the participants' lived experiences (Finlay 2009; Moustakas 1994; Ponterotto 2005). A phenomenological study begins with a "fresh and unbiased description of the subject matter" (Wertz 2005, 167) and attempts to "see into the heart of things" (van Manen 2007, 12). Phenomenologists describe rather than explain (Moustakas 1994; Whiting 2002). Phenomenological research captures a depth of understanding about the meaning of human experiences through an iterative process of open-minded exploration and discovery (Moustakas 1994). The phenomenological approach is philosophical in nature and derives key elements from the writings of Husserl, Heidegger, and Sartre (Creswell 2013). Key philosophical elements of phenomenology include "the intentionality of consciousness" and the rejection of "subject-object dichotomies" (Creswell 2013, 79–80). These philosophical concepts maintain that an individual's personal perspective, experience, and awareness of an object define that reality. A phenomenological study incorporates both what has been experienced and how it has been experienced and searches for the essence of the phenomenon shared among those who have experienced it (Creswell 2013; Moustakas 1994). Wertz (2005) described phenomenology as "an in-dwelling, meditative philosophy that glories in the concreteness of person-world relations and accords lived experience, with all its ambiguity, primacy over the known" (p. 175).

Through a process of in-depth interviews and inquiries, the researcher looked for themes that were common to those who have experienced the phenomenon. The researcher, the participants, and the dialogue are the instruments of the research, and the findings are in the form of words and narratives rather than numbers (Goulding 2005). The process is inductive, and the identification of themes and broad concepts takes place through the analysis of the participant's stories and reflections. By exploring the extent of an individual's experience, a phenomenological approach can provide insights into "the complexities of human life and the fullness of our experience of it" (Gibson & Hanes 2003, 182). Documenting the experiences, feelings, concerns, and reactions of women who have overcome gender discrimination may illuminate gender-based stereotypes, biases, and behaviors, and provide the insights needed to eliminate them. A constructivist phenomenological study that describes the impact of gender bias on women as they strive to achieve their academic and career goals could promote understanding and lead to needed social change (Brooks & Nagy Hesse-Biber 2007). It is important to gain a deeper understanding of the lived experiences of the small percentage of women who have broken through the glass ceiling by using buffering behaviors in STEM professions. The knowledge gained through this phenomenological study provides insights and understandings of what women experience as they overcome gender discrimination and become senior leaders in male-dominated fields.

Quantitative methods were rejected for this study primarily because the positivist paradigms of quantitative research assume there is a single reality, formulate a hypothesis a priori, and then use statistical tools to collect evidence to either prove or disprove the theory postulated. These methods would not be appropriate for this study since the inquiry focuses on understanding the distinct human experiences of individuals, and there is no theory to prove or disprove. A qualitative research design was determined to be more appropriate since there are multiple realities, and the participants determine these realities through their experiences and not through quantifiable measurements.

Appropriateness of Methodology

A phenomenological approach is appropriate for this study as it recognizes and honors the validity of the human experience to inform concepts that lead to understanding (Groenewald 2004; van Manen 2007). This methodology will expand the knowledge of women's experiences of seeking leadership by using an iterative process of open-minded exploration and discovery (Gibson & Hanes 2003). Feminist phenomenological methodology positions women at the center of the research design, elevates the power of the individual's experience, and describes the underlying themes of those who have lived in the situation (Brooks & Hesse-Biber 2007; Landman 2006). Feminist epistemology specifically addresses who can be a source of knowledge, what can be known, and how it can be known (Landman 2006). The feminist phenomenological approach, which makes the lived experiences of women central to discovery of knowledge, offsets the historical exclusion of women's knowledge from positivist scientific research (Stanley & Wise 1993). Feminists view phenomenology as an effective way to introduce an egalitarian methodology in which there is recognition that participants have power and knowledge and that research findings can promote social change and overcome the historical marginalization of women and their views (Kasper 1994; Landman 2006).

Feminist research has as its goal the transformation of current practices to create gender equity and moral fairness (Brooks & Hesse-Biber 2007; Creswell 2013; Fisher 2000; Martin 2003). This approach starts with a phenomenon that is of great interest or is an "abiding concern" to the researcher (Creswell 2013, 79). The data from this study can inform and enlighten those who are presently in positions of power and making senior leadership selection decisions. A critical consequence would be to ensure a sustainable, diverse, competent workforce that is necessary to be competitive in a global market, particularly in the fields of science, technology, engineering, and mathematics.

This feminist phenomenological study maintains that there are populations whose voices either have been ignored or suppressed (Martin 2003; Ponterotto 2005). The goal of this study was to capture the voices of women who have struggled with the disparity of power based on gender (Brooks & Hesse-Biber 2007). A phenomenological exploration of gender discrimination has the potential to shed light on an area of social and organizational injustice that needs to be corrected (Ehrich 2005). The phenomenologist argues that the only way to know the truth of a situation is through the eyes of those who have lived it—only then can one derive the common themes that constitute the basic essence of truth (Finlay 2009; Gibson & Hanes 2003; Groenewald 2004; Whiting 2002).

Beliefs and Worldviews of the Researcher

One of the distinctive aspects of phenomenology is the requirement that the researcher first identifies and then attempts to keep separate any of her preconceived ideas about the phenomenon in order to see the situation totally through the lived experiences of the participants. This activity is described as bracketing (Whiting 2002), or reflexivity (Creswell 2013). Bracketing or reflexivity takes place throughout all stages of data analysis in order to make known to the researcher, and eventually to the reader, the researcher's views, perspectives, and experiences related to the phenomenon. The goal is to reduce the possibility that the viewing lens of the researcher may distort the data (Whiting 2002). The goal of pure objectivity is not humanly possible, but the exercise of bracketing brings these issues to the conscious awareness of the researcher and the reader (Tufford 2000).

The author is an executive coach and works with women who hold senior leadership positions in the STEM professions, many of whom have encountered gender bias and backlash in their career progression. Discussions in coaching sessions often center on developing strategies and responses to issues of institutionalized gender bias. I also served as the vice president of organizational development for a worldwide major hotel chain, and was the only female senior executive throughout my nine-year tenure. I encountered gender bias but found ways to overcome these obstacles and became an advocate for equal opportunities for women and minorities. I am a mentor and adviser for the Society for Women in Engineering and for the Women's Innovation Network.

The author is the only female member on the board of directors of a global engineering firm of scientists, technologists, engineers, and researchers. Gender disparity in leadership selection is widespread in the firm, and the researcher advocates for leadership selection practices that ensure gender equity and proportional representation of highly qualified women at the senior leadership level. The author's interest in the topic of women's leadership led to the selection of a feminist critical advocacy approach for this research.

The author sought to maintain a bias-free approach to the study by keeping a reflexivity journal in which she captured her impressions, beliefs, and reactions to the phenomenon during the study. She engaged in dialogue with colleagues outside of the research study to calibrate any reactions she experienced and attempted to filter them out of the research (Tufford 2000). Prior to data collection and throughout data analysis, the researcher conducted subjectivity audits (Peshkin 1988). Preconceptions at one stage of data analysis may carry over to subsequent stages, so identifying subjectivity was ongoing (Tufford 2000).

Research Questions

In qualitative research, the research questions identify the phenomenon of interest and help to focus the direction of the study (Ryan, Coughlan, & Cronin 2007). The central research question guiding this study will be:

CR1:   What are the lived experiences of women in
         STEM senior leadership using buffering be-
         haviors to overcome gender bias and achieve
         success?

The following questions will further support this study:

1. What are women's perceptions and experiences of impression
   management as a buffering behavior against gender bias and
   backlash?
2. What are women's perceptions and experiences of political skill
   as a buffering behavior against gender bias and backlash?
3. What are women's perceptions and experiences of self-
   monitoring as a buffering behavior against gender bias and
   backlash?
4. What are women's perceptions and experiences of performance
   as a buffering behavior against gender bias and backlash?

Selection of Participants

Phenomenological research explores the lived experiences or the in-
sider's view of an experience or phenomenon. The primary criterion is
the suitability of the participant rather than the numerical predictive
validity of a large group. The author selected participants because they
had a story to tell that may help describe the phenomenon under investigation. Selection criteria for qualitative studies are primarily the quality of the story rather than the quantity of the individuals selected for
the study. When selecting participants for a phenomenological study,
the task is to find and select individuals who report having experienced
the phenomenon under study. The critical question that the researcher
needs to ask is, "Does this participant have the experience that I am
looking for?" (Englander 2012, 19).

The author selected study participants who had exposure to or experience with using buffering behaviors to overcome gender bias to reach senior leadership positions in STEM. This type of sampling is known as purposive or purposeful (Fosse, Harvey, McDermott, & Davidson 2002). This approach differs from quantitative sampling in that participants are selected based on their ability to purposefully inform the area under study (Creswell 2013). Since the goal of phenomenological research is to collect extensive detail to describe the essence of a phenomenon, the researcher recruited individuals that could provide in-depth and personal knowledge of the phenomenon. To determine whether potential participants had lived experiences with the phenomenon of buffering behaviors, participants completed a four-question, binary scale preselection questionnaire. The questionnaire is in appendix B.

The participants in this study consisted of sixteen women who hold advanced academic degrees in science, technology, engineering, and mathematics, work within the STEM professions, and have attained senior leadership positions in medium- to large-size North American organizations, primarily in the northeastern United States. A participant pool of sixteen was chosen for the research because studies have shown that data saturation occurs in qualitative studies of relatively homogeneous groups of participants within twelve interviews, and that as few as six interviews generated common themes (Guest, Bunce, & Johnson 2006; Mason 2010). Englander (2012) pointed out that an emphasis on sample size corresponds to a quantitative research methodology in which generalizability requires large sample sizes. Generalizability is not the goal of qualitative studies, and Englander (2012) believed a discussion of sample size in qualitative research is irrelevant but recommends that a researcher use at least three participants (p. 20). In order to understand the common experience, the selection process for study participants used homogenous purposeful sampling to ensure that all participants had experienced the phenomenon being explored (Fosse, Harvey, McDermott, & Davidson 2002).

Potential participants for the study were identified through personal and professional networks of colleagues, peers, and acquaintances and through direct mail contact with the researcher's client organizations in the STEM field as well as the Women's Innovation Network and the Society of Women Engineers. The women who volunteered to participate in the study recommended other potential participants. The selection criteria included (a) women who are in senior leadership positions in science, technology, engineering, or mathematics and (b) have encountered and overcome gender-based obstacles in their careers. Potential participants have a minimum of three years in their leadership role and have decision-making authority over others. Senior leadership is defined as a director, vice president, senior vice president, or executive vice president. Also included are the positions of CEO, CFO, COO, and CIO.

Face-to-face conversations were used to contact potential participants, describe the purpose of the study and ascertain interest. When a potential participant indicated an interest in participating, the individual completed a brief screening questionnaire (see appendix B) to determine if they met the criterion for the study.

Information explaining what the study would entail was provided to all qualified individuals who indicated an interest in participating in the study so they could arrive at a well-informed decision regarding whether or not to participate in the research. Individuals who elected to participate in the study completed a written consent form and were assigned a unique identifier code to ensure anonymity. To further ensure anonymity and confidentiality, the signed consent form, the identity and contact information of participants, participants' organizational and professional affiliation and demographics are kept in confidence and not mentioned anywhere in the study. This study did involve human subjects; however, none of the participants were under eighteen years old, mentally handicapped, imprisoned, or considered a member of a vulnerable population. All participants for this voluntary study are (a) senior professional women in science, technology, engineering, and mathematics who were contacted through personal and professional networks of colleagues and peers and (b) other qualified women recommended by participants who agreed to participate in the study.

Data Collection

There is only one valid source of data in a phenomenological study and that source is the participant (Gibson & Hanes 2003). The phenomenologist contends that to understand the meaning of a human experience, one must reject the natural science model that creates abstract theories about phenomenon and look instead to the experience of the human being about the phenomenon (DeCastro 2003). The underlying assumption is that common themes may exist within the shared lived experiences and that these themes can be articulated. The goal is to understand the meaning of the phenomenon by collecting the narratives from individuals who have shared the experience (Englander 2012). Interviews that elicited participants' stories, perceptions, feelings, opinions, and beliefs about their experiences with using buffering behaviors to overcome gender discrimination were the focal point of data collection in this study. Phenomenological interviewing is based on the philosophical view that the essence and meaning of a phenomenon can be known through the accounts of lived experiences from individuals who have lived through or are living in the phenomenon. The criterion for an effective phenomenological research interview is "as complete a description as possible of the experience the participant has lived through" (Giorgi 2009, 122). In order to use phenomenological interviewing effectively, the researcher adopted an unstructured state of mind during data collection and was open to emerging evidence that may suggest new avenues of exploration. Since the primary data collection instrument in qualitative research is the researcher, it was essential that she accurately record the experiences, reflections, insights, and observations that research participants shared (Lewis 2009).

The phenomenological interview process and the subsequent interpretation of the interview material recognized "the temporal and transitory nature of the human experience, subjective understanding, lived experience as the foundation of the phenomena, and the emphasis on meaning and meaning in context" (Seidman 2013, 17–18). Seidman (2013) proposed a three-stage interview model for phenomenological inquiry. The first stage is a "focused life history" (Seidman 2013, 21) that inquires about experiences from the participant's past. The second stage focuses on the details of the participant's experiences in the present, and the third stage asks the participant to reflect on the meaning of her experiences with the phenomenon (Seidman 2013). Prior to interviewing, the researcher used a similar three-stage process to describe her own experience with the phenomenon in order to bracket or separate her experiences from the participants' and to discover and separate out any preconception that the researcher may have (Seidman 2013). The three-stage interview model took place within a sixty- to ninety-minute face-to-face or telephone interview. The interviews took place in the participant's private office or another place of her choosing where she felt comfortable. Interviews took place in quiet, private, and distraction-free environments. One interview was conducted by telephone, and an e-mail was sent to the participant containing a call-in number and meeting ID. A written consent form was obtained prior to all interviews.

In a qualitative phenomenological study, the researcher must ensure that the phenomenon continues to be the focus of the dialogue (Landman 2006). The researcher accomplished this by conducting face-to-face and telephone in-depth interviews consisting of open-ended questions emanating from the research questions. The researcher remained flexible enough to allow for the exploration of additional factors or issues that emerged and that encouraged narration of the participant's stories and experiences. Free listing is an interview technique that can help to identify important themes that lead to the essence of the phenomenon. In free listing, the researcher asked participants to identify all the factors or issues that contributed to their experiences of overcoming gender discrimination and then to discuss these experiences according to importance or significance (Patton & Cochran 2002). Another phenomenological interviewing approach asks the participant to recall critical incidents, turning points, or significant decisions that may have been a result of the phenomenon under study (Patton & Cochran 2002). Moustakas (1994) suggested that the core of the phenomenological interview consist of two broad questions such as, "What have your experiences been in terms of the phenomenon?" and "What situations or contexts have influenced or affected your experiences of the phenomenon?" These two questions ensure that the phenomenon is described both texturally and contextually, thereby more completely describing the common experiences of participants. The researcher asked participants to describe their experiences both texturally and contextually with the use of buffering behaviors to overcome gender bias as they earned advanced degrees and achieved high-level leadership positions in their organizations.

The researcher utilized a script that began with an explanation of the study and a request for the participant's consent. The researcher provided a consent form to each participant and interviewing did not begin until the participant read and signed the consent form and returned it to the researcher. The researcher audio-recorded all interviews. The researcher interviewed all participants for approximately sixty to ninety minutes and recorded the interviews with the permission of the participant. After the interviews, the researcher had the recordings professionally transcribed verbatim and housed the transcripts in confidential computer files. The researcher made daily backups of the files. The researcher took all appropriate precautions to ensure that neither the participant nor her company is identifiable in any report. Company locations, products, brands, and/or corporate activities are being kept strictly confidential. Throughout the study, the researcher was highly cognizant of potential ethical issues and/or harm to subjects and employed all appropriate procedures to minimize the risks. Descriptions of the roles of participants do not contain any identifying data or information. Pseudonyms are used throughout the data report.

Data Analysis

The analysis of data in a phenomenological study is cyclical, iterative, descriptive, emergent, and intertwined with data collection (Creswell 2013; Giorgi 2009; Whiting 2002). The goal of data analysis in a qualitative phenomenological study is to describe as accurately as possible the common themes, the broad concepts, and the fundamental essence of a shared phenomenon by recording, coding, and analyzing the lived experiences of individuals who have personal knowledge of the phenomenon. Giorgi used four principal characteristics to describe phenomenological data analysis. These characteristics require that data analysis (a) be descriptive, (b) use reduction, (c) search for essences, and (d) focus on intentionality (De Castro 2003, 49).

This phenomenological study describes the lived experiences of women who have overcome gender-based barriers and become leaders in the male-dominated fields of science, technology, engineering, and mathematics. The central research question was, "What are the lived experiences of women in STEM senior leadership using buffering behaviors to overcome gender bias and achieve success?" The goal was to discover and describe thematic categories that offer insight into the events that the participants consider significant as they rose to senior leadership positions in the male-dominated science and engineering professions. From this data, the researcher identified common themes regarding the essence of the phenomenon from the factual narratives of the participants' lived experiences of gender bias.

In qualitative research, data analysis begins at the outset of the study (Thorne 2000). As the researcher constructs the first question for the first interview and records the responses, data analysis is taking place. As the researcher listens to, processes, and makes sense of the information participants share, analysis is taking place. Data analysis is present as early as research design, the literature review, and data collection and continues through to the writing of the findings (Thorne 2000). The instruments of data collection and data analysis in phenomenological studies include the researcher, the participants, and the participants' stories and reflections. Findings consist of themes and broad concepts and are expressed in a unifying narrative rather than in numbers (Goulding 2005).

Open-ended questions that are flexible enough to allow for alternative avenues of inquiry and the exploration of additional themes that may emerge guided this study. The organization of interview notes is also a preliminary data analysis step since the organization of notes requires decisions on the part of the researcher (Bailey 2008).

The basic components in qualitative data analysis are (a) identifying units of meaning, (b) grouping units of meaning into themes, and (c) pinpointing general and unique themes (Atkinson, Coffey, Delamont & Hammersly 2005, 406). This study used Giorgi's four-step process of data analysis from his Scientific Phenomenological Psychological Method (2009, 128–137) and Saldaña's first cycle and second cycle coding processes (Saldaña 2012).

Step 1: Read for a Sense of the Whole

Attribute coding provided context for the data analysis performed in step 1 by describing the setting in which the study took place, the participant demographics and salient characteristics, the data collection format, and the time frame within which the data were collected (Saldaña 2012). In this first step, the researcher read the entire set of transcriptions to get a sense of the whole and to understand what the description is about (Giorgi 2009, 126). One of the distinctive aspects of phenomenology is the requirement that the researcher first identify and then attempt to keep separate any of her preconceived ideas about the phenomenon in order to see the situation totally through the lived experiences of the participants. This activity is bracketing and begins with reflexivity; the examination of a researcher's preconceived notions and beliefs about the phenomenon.

Reflexivity and bracketing took place throughout all stages of data analysis in order to make known to the researcher and eventually to the reader, the researcher's views, perspectives, and experiences related to the phenomenon, thereby reducing the possibility that data analysis may be distorted by the viewing lens of the researcher (Whiting 2002). Pure objectivity is not humanly possible, but the exercise of bracketing brings these issues to the conscious awareness of the researcher and the reader (Tufford 2000). The researcher accomplished this by including her own impressions, beliefs, and reactions to the phenomenon throughout the memoing process. She kept a reflexivity journal in which she captured her reactions and preconceptions to the research process and engaged in dialogue with colleagues outside of the research to calibrate any reactions she was experiencing and filtering them out of the research (Tufford 2000). Prior to beginning data collection and throughout the data analysis process, the researcher conducted subjectivity audits in order to identify areas of potential subjectivity (Peshkin 1988). Since preconceptions that surface at any one stage of data analysis may carry over to subsequent stages, identifying areas of subjectivity was ongoing (Tufford 2000).

Step 2: Determination of Meaning Units

In step 2 of data analysis, the researcher read each transcript in its entirety several times and began to identify recurring elements (Giorgi 2009; Whiting 2002). The process of phenomenological reduction or de-contextualizing removes units of text from their source while keeping their meaning intact (Burnard 1994). These segments of text are the meaning units (Burnard 1994). Meaning units can be phrases, sentences, or a series of sentences and are separate entities that convey one idea, one episode, or one piece of information (Burnard 1994; Welsch 2002). The first cycle coding method in step 2 of data analysis used in vivo coding, which utilizes the participant's actual words to create codes. As such, in vivo coding is particularly useful when the researcher wishes to honor the voices of the participants (Saldaña 2012). In vivo coding also ensures that the first cycle codes are generated by participant experience rather than researcher interpretation. When reading the interview transcripts, the researcher noted the words and phrases that were vocally emphasized, often repeated, or seemed to carry particular emotional weight and used these verbal elements to create codes. This process of interacting with the text and identifying individual elements of the participant's lived experience organizes the data for second cycle analysis and coding (Giorgi 2009; Jones 2007; Saldaña 2012). As meaning units or textual segments were identified, they were coded using actual words or phrases that are descriptive of discrete elements from the participant's lived experiences. The researcher then identified the theme that stands out in each unit and listed them (Groenewald 2004; Saldaña 2012). Themeing the data is a process in which the meaning of a unit of data is explained in a phrase or a sentence (Saldaña 2012). Themeing the data is particularly applicable to phenomenological studies and can provide insight into the essential elements and meanings of the experience and eventually lead to metathemes (Saldaña 2012). This process of recontextualizing or themeing the data collected the meaning units into categories that began to describe the essence of the phenomenon (Giorgi 2009; Jones 2007; Saldaña 2012). It was through this process of decontextualizing, coding, and recontextualizing that the data became useful and illuminated the phenomenon (Basit 2003; Giorgi 2009; Jones 2007).

The researcher utilized the software program NVivo 7.0 to analyze the data and assist in classifying, sorting, and coding information. NVivo 7.0 software also assisted in identifying unifying themes.

Step 3: Interrogating the Data and Transforming Meaning Units into Phenomenological and Psychological Expressions

In this stage of data analysis, as before, the researcher must acknowledge and set aside any preconceived ideas or beliefs about the phenomenon. This stage involves in-depth questioning of the data collected in the previous stage and asking, "What does this tell me about women's experiences with buffering behaviors in overcoming gender bias as they seek senior leadership positions in male-dominated STEM?" The researcher examined both the meaning units and the themes in light of the phenomenon. Giorgi describes this step as "interrogating each meaning unit to discover how to express in a more satisfactory way the psychological implications of the lifeworld description" (Giorgi 2009, 131). Step 3 of data analysis utilized the second cycle coding method known as pattern coding, in which overarching themes are identified and metacodes are developed (Saldaña 2012). Most computer assisted qualitative data analysis software(CAQDAS) programs include an application that performs "super coding" that will review the first cycle codes and provide pattern codes (Saldaña 2012; Wickham & Woods 2005). If certain units and central themes emerge repeatedly across all interviews, the researcher will identify these areas as final themes or revelatory themes (Whiting 2002). Anderson describes this stage as a form of "low hovering" (2007, 1) over the data. The goal is to identify those clusters of themes that "give expression to the communality of voices across participants" (Anderson 2007, 1). In preparation for step 4, structural synthesis, the researcher created "categories of categories" (Saldaña 2012, 250). These metacategories formed the basis of the unifying elements of the phenomenon as described by participants.

Step 4: Structural Synthesis

After a thorough examination of the identified phenomenological themes, the researcher composed a unifying statement that tied together the "essential non-redundant themes" (Whiting 2002, 69). Creswell calls this the "culminating aspect" of the phenomenological study (2013, 194). This stage of data analysis examines and integrates the data describing what the participants experienced and how they experienced it in order to describe the meaning and essence of the phenomenon for those individuals (Creswell 2013; Moustakas 1994). The researcher transformed these meaning unit, themes, and categories into "psychologically pertinent expressions (Giorgi 2009, 137). However, the cyclical nature of phenomenological data analysis requires that the researcher revisit each of the four stages and allow for additional insights, ideas, and inspirations to emerge.

Ensuring Research Quality

This study incorporated Creswell's (2013) suggestions for ensuring quality in qualitative research. Specifically, the study attempted to (a) illustrate the philosophical foundation of phenomenology, (b) clearly articulate the phenomenon under study, (c) utilize recognized phenomenological procedures, (d) convey the essence of the participants' lived experiences, and (e) include reflexivity disclosures. The issues of validity for qualitative research differ from those of quantitative research. Quantitative research starts with a hypothesis and then uses a variety of statistical tools and measurements to determine causality.

It is a deductive process and relies heavily on numbers. Qualitative research uses field research to collect and understand lived experiences of subjects and then inductively looks for common themes or explanations for the observations. The primary validity focus or concern in qualitative research is the researcher and his or her data collection methods.

The validity questions that are important in qualitative research focus on whether the researcher actually observes what he or she thinks he or she has observed, whether the researcher has collected, recorded, and reported data accurately, and whether the researcher has accurately represented the lived experiences and meanings that the study's participants intended (Creswell 2013). To achieve a "confluence of evidence that breeds credibility" (Creswell 2013, 246) the researcher incorporated the following strategies into the study:

1. The researcher conducted prolonged field engagement in order to build trust with participants and determine what is relevant to the study.
2. Data collection incorporated triangulation, a method of seeking corroborating evidence through other researchers, sources, and theories.
3. The researcher enlisted a peer debriefer to challenge the researcher's interpretations of data, theme assessments, and conclusions.
4. The data analysis stage utilized "member checking" sessions In member checking, the researcher reviews the data with the participants and determines whether they agree with it or if they feel modifications are needed (Creswell 2013).
5. Detailed accounts that incorporate extensive layers of situational facts as well as the feelings, impressions, perceptions, thoughts, and reactions of the participants ensure rich, thick

descriptions. It is through this level of descriptiveness that the reader will determine if transferability of findings is possible.

Ethical Assurances

The researcher complied with all ethical principles and guidelines for the protection of participants developed by the National Commission for the Protection of Human Subjects of Biomedical and Behavioral Research. The researcher studied *The Belmont Report: Ethical Principles and Guidelines for the Protection of Human Subjects of Research* and the US Department of Health and Human Services (HHS) regulations 45 CFR 46, Subpart A, known as The Common Rule, and will incorporate these protections into the design and execution of this research study. Specifically, the researcher:

1. Ensured that all participants had the choice to participate in or decline to participate in the research and assured participants that their choice will not result in any special consequences. The researcher informed participants of their right to withdraw from the research at any time or to decline to answer any questions posed to them. The researcher provided sufficient information about the scope, content, and requirements of participant participation so potential participants could make an informed decision.

2. Implemented measures that protected participants from harm. Risks to participants were minimal and were further reduced by ensuring confidentiality of the participants' identities, their participation in the research, their organizational affiliation, or any identifying characteristics that might lead to discovery of a participant's identity.

Potential concerns regarding two specific areas in this study include recruitment of participants and the fact that the researcher plans to use participants from client organizations. The researcher used snowball sampling to identify participants. Snowball sampling is a technique in which the researcher asks research participants to identify others who may have experienced the phenomena under study so that the researcher may invite the suggested individual to join the study. To ameliorate concerns regarding the use of snowball sampling compromising a potential participant's privacy, the researcher provided information about the study and suggested that she contact the researcher if interested in participating in the study. The risk to participants in this study is minimal, however the researcher accepts that if certain others discovered a participant's identify, there is the potential of economic risk.

APA Section 8.04, the use of "Client/Patient, Student, and Subordinate Research Participants," may pose another concern. The researcher, through her association as an executive coach with client organizations, knows several of the participants. However, the researcher is not in a position to grant or withhold any positive or negative consequences to these potential participants. The researcher adhered to stringent guidelines of confidentiality to protect both the identity of the participants and the organizations.

The following sections of the APA Code of Ethics also applied to the research:

APA Section 4.07

"Use of Confidential Information for Didactic or Other Purposes," prohibits psychologists from "disclosing personally identifiable information concerning their research participant unless they take reasonable steps to disguise the person or organization, or the person or organization has consented in writing" (American Psychological Association

2002, 7). The researcher has taken all reasonable steps to disguise both
the participant's identity and the identity of the organization.

APA Section 6.02

"Maintenance, Dissemination, and Disposal of Confidential Records of
Professional and Scientific Work" requires that "psychologists maintain
confidentiality in creating, storing, accessing, transferring, and dispos-
ing of records under their control, whether these are written, auto-
mated, or in any other medium" (American Psychological Association
2002, 8–9). The researcher utilized security measures to ensure confidentiality of data, records, notes, and audio recordings.

APA Section 8.04

"Client/Patient, Student, and Subordinate Research Participants," requires that "when psychologists conduct research with clients/patients,
students, or subordinates as participants, psychologists take steps to
protect the prospective participants from adverse consequences of de-
clining or withdrawing from participation" (American Psychological
Association 2002, 10). Several of the prospective participants are members of client organizations of the researcher. The researcher thoroughly described the goals of the research and emphasized that participation in the study is voluntary. The researcher also stressed that
the participant could withdraw from the study at any time without
consequence and could choose not to answer any questions.

APA Section 8.08

"Debriefing" requires that "psychologists provide a prompt opportunity for participants to obtain appropriate information about the nature, results, and conclusions of the research, and they take reasonable

steps to correct any misconceptions that participants may have of which the psychologists are aware" (American Psychological Association 2002, 11). The researcher included in her member checking interviews the opportunity to debrief each participant and correct any misunderstandings or misperceptions that may have resulted from the research as well as offer access to appropriate resources if participants experienced stress as a result of the interview process.

Institutional Review Board: Potential Concerns and Ethical Issues

Both the Common Rule and the Belmont Report require that any study that includes research with human subjects must be reviewed. The term research is defined as a "systematic investigation designed to develop or contribute to generalizable knowledge" and human subject means "a living individual about whom the researcher obtains data through intervention or interaction or identifiable private information" (Belmont Report 1979). The design of this study met both definitions of research and human subject.

Summary

Despite the strides that women have made in earning advanced degrees in science, technology, engineering, and mathematics and achieving senior leadership positions in corporate organizations, there is significant evidence that the barriers to advancement based on gender bias and discrimination are firmly in place. This phenomenological study was designed to discover, understand, and describe the meaning and essence of the lived experiences of women in the fields of science, technology, engineering, and mathematics in using buffering behaviors to overcome gender bias and backlash to reach the upper levels of leadership.

A phenomenological approach is appropriate for this study as it recognizes and honors the validity of the human experience to inform concepts that lead to understanding (Groenewald 2004; van Manen 2007). A phenomenological study elevates the power of the individual's worldview and describes the underlying themes shared by those who have also experienced the phenomenon (Moustakas 1994). A phenomenological study provides important insights into the meaning of a phenomenon and an understanding that these experiences could be valuable for organizational leaders at all levels. By giving voice to the pioneering women who have met these challenges with courage, tenacity, and grace, the researcher hopes that aspiring women and other marginalized populations will find encouragement to continue to strive to reach their career goals.

CHAPTER 4

Findings

The purpose of this phenomenological study was to explore the essence and meaning of the lived experiences of senior women leaders who have used buffering behaviors to overcome gender-based barriers and achieve positions of leadership in the traditionally male-dominated fields of science, technology, engineering, or mathematics (STEM). Chapter 4 presents the key findings from interviews with sixteen participants who hold senior leadership positions in STEM organizations in the United States, all of whom reported successfully employing buffering behaviors to overcome gender bias and discrimination. The researcher identified recurring themes and patterns that illuminate the phenomenon of the use of buffering behaviors of women confronting gender-based bias and achieving leadership roles in STEM. The data also revealed themes and patterns that illustrate and expand upon the conceptual framework described in chapter 3.

This design focuses exclusively on the views and experiences of women who have encountered discrimination and marginalization based on their gender and persevered to attain positions of leadership in STEM organizations. Chapter 4 provides demographic information of the participants, a review of the data collection process, the methodology used in data analysis, and the themes that emerged from the data. Themes are presented in the context of the study's theoretical and conceptual frameworks, the pertinent literature on the theme, and the central research question.

Theoretical and Conceptual Frameworks

This study is set within the theoretical framework of Bandura's social cognitive theory (Bandura 1994, 2001; Bandura, Caprara, Barbaranelli, Gerbino, & Pastorelli 2003; Bussey & Bandura 1999; Chen 2006), which holds that individuals can consciously learn and choose behaviors that will influence outcomes within their environments. Bandura's social cognitive theory (2001) is central to the entire study as it describes the concept of self-efficacy. This foundational theory served as a lens through which the researcher examined and analyzed the data collected, both from the literature and from the participants. Two aspects of social cognitive theory, self-regulation and self-efficacy, emerged as essential components of success for the women in the study. Self-regulation is defined as the ability to "perceive, evaluate and regulate behavior" and self-efficacy is described as "people's beliefs in their capabilities to produce desired effects by their own actions" (Bandura 2001, 10).

The conceptual framework of this study is presented in three main areas: (a) the role of self-efficacy in the use of buffering behaviors, (b) the gender-based barriers that the participants encountered in STEM that created the need for buffering behaviors, and (c) examples of the buffering behaviors women employed to overcome these barriers. The sources of self-efficacy and the use of self-efficacious behaviors provide important insights into the beliefs and actions that sustained the women in the study as they confronted gender bias and marginalization. The conceptual elements of masculine hegemony, gender bias, gender backlash, and gendered organizations frame the experiences of gender-based hostility, barriers, and obstacles encountered by the women in the study. The results juxtapose examples of the challenges women encountered against the buffering behaviors they utilized to overcome these challenges with self-monitoring, impression management, political skill, and performance.

The first conceptual area, self-efficacy, provides examples of early messages and experiences that helped to shape women's beliefs of self-efficacy. The data collected on self-efficacy is presented in two subcategories, each of which produced two themes for a total of four self-efficacy-related themes.

The second conceptual area, gender-based barriers, begins with data from the lived experiences of the participants that reveals the effects of the masculine construction of leadership, which incorporates gendered stereotypes of leadership and masculine hegemony. The next gender-based barrier, gender bias, is illustrated through the stories that women shared of encountering derogatory comments, gender slurs, and discriminatory actions that appeared to stem from being a woman in a male-dominated profession. Related to gender bias is the third category of gender-based barriers, gender backlash (Garcia-Retamero & Lopez-Zafra 2006; Heilman, Wallen, Fuchs, & Tamkins 2004; O'Neill & O'Reilly 2011). The participants recount numerous examples of gender backlash. As women rose to positions of leadership, they recalled reactions from male colleagues who denigrated their achievements and sought to make success difficult. The fourth gender-based barrier in the conceptual framework draws from gender schema theories (Lemons & Parzinger 2007) and theories of gendered organizations (Acker 2006; Ridgeway 2009). Women seeking positions of leadership in male-dominated professions often encounter cultural "inequality regimes" (Acker 2006, 443) and report that they do not feel as though they fit and do not belong (Wentling & Thomas 2009).

The third main category of the conceptual framework, buffering behaviors, describes how women overcame gender-based barriers by developing and utilizing efficacious responses and strategies. The buffering behaviors described in this study include self-monitoring (Gupta 2013; O'Neill & O'Reilly 2011), impression management (Hirshfield 2011; O'Neill & O'Reilly 2011), political skill (Shaughnessy, Treadway, Breland, Williams, & Brouer 2011), and performance (Jalbert, Jalbert, & Furumo 2013).

Research Question

The following central research question guided this study: What are the lived experiences of women in STEM senior leadership using buffering behaviors to overcome gender bias and achieve success? In qualitative research, the central research question is designed to be as broad as possible in order to explore the phenomena in a wide-ranging and comprehensive way (Creswell 2002). Ohman (2005) suggested that qualitative questions allow "informants to tell their story" (p. 275). In addition to the central research question, subquestions explored the specific gender-based barriers that women encountered and the buffering behaviors they utilized to overcome gender discrimination. The interview questions maintained elements of open-endedness and neutral language but secondary probing did elicit greater specificity for understanding the central question (Creswell 2002).

Participants

When selecting participants for a phenomenological study, the task is to recruit individuals who can provide in-depth and personal knowledge of the phenomenon. The critical question that the researcher must ask is, "Does this participant have the experience that I am looking for?" (Englander 2012, 19). The researcher identified participants for the study through personal and professional networks of colleagues, clients, peers, and acquaintances and through direct e-mail contact with the researcher's client organizations in the STEM field. The researcher also contacted members of two organizations, the Women's Innovation Network and the Society of Women Engineers. The participants in the study were all volunteers. The selection criteria included (a) women who are in senior leadership positions in science, technology, engineering, or mathematics; and (b) have encountered and overcome gender-based obstacles in their careers. To determine whether potential participants possessed lived experiences of the phenomenon of buffering behaviors, participants completed a four-question, preselection questionnaire. The questionnaire is in appendix B. The researcher selected study participants who had exposure to or experience with buffering behaviors in overcoming gender bias and have personally reached senior leadership positions in STEM. This type of sampling is known as purposive or purposeful (Fosse, Harvey, McDermott, & Davidson 2002).

Sixteen women from the fields of and backgrounds in science, technology, engineering, and mathematics completed the screening questionnaire and were selected to participate in this study.

Table 1

Participant Demographics

Participant	Degree (s)	Field	Title
Alice	MD, MSc	Internal Medicine; Translational Research	VP
Amy	MS	Chemistry	SVP
Ann	MD	Radiation Oncology	Medical Director
Claire	MS	Environmental Sciences	VP
Dale	MSSE	Structural Engineering	Senior Structural Engineer
Gina	MD	Medicine	VP
Jennifer	BS; PE	Environmental Engineering	SVP
Kate	MS	Civil Engineering	VP
Karen	BS	Accounting	Owner/Partner
Mary	PhD	Systems Engineering	SVP
Randi	MS (2), BS	Electrical Engineering Civil Engineering IT Systems Design and Management	Senior Project Manager
Sabine	MS	Hydrogeology	Senior Project Manager
Susan	MD; MSc	Medicine	Medical Director
Tess	MD, MSc	Medical Research; Immunology	VP
Vivian	MD; PhD	Internal Medicine; Endocrinology & Metabolic Disease	Director Medical Research
Yasmin	BS	Industrial Engineering	Senior Project Manager

Note. To protect confidentiality, all names used in this table and throughout the study are pseudonyms.

Five of the participants hold medical degrees, one participant holds both an MD and PhD degree, one participant holds a PhD in systems engineering, six have master's degrees (one in structural engineering, one in geotechnical engineering, one in systems design and management, one in chemistry, one in environmental sciences, and one in geology), three hold bachelor's degrees in civil and/or environmental engineering and are certified professional engineers, and one is a CPA who owns her own business. Participants all had a minimum of three years in their leadership role and have decision-making authority over others.

The ages of the participants range from thirty-four to sixty-four. One participant was within the age range of thirty to thirty-five; one was between thirty-five and forty years of age; four participants were between forty-one and forty-five years of age; two participants were between forty-six and fifty years of age; three participants were between fifty-one and fifty-five years of age; three participants were between fifty-six and sixty years of age, and two participants were sixty-one years old or older. Participants in the field of engineering hold undergraduate and graduate degrees in geotechnical engineering, civil engineering, electrical engineering, environmental engineering, structural engineering, and industrial engineering. Participants in the field of medical science hold degrees in physiology, neurology, immunology, internal medicine, oncology, endocrinology, microbiology, and metabolic sciences. Mathematics degrees included applied mathematics and economics; technical degrees included operational business intelligence, systems design, accounting, and environmental planning. Of the sixteen participants, fourteen presently hold leadership positions in global STEM organizations. Two of the participants own and lead consulting firms that serve STEM organizations. The participants' years of professional experience in STEM ranged from fifteen to thirty-two years. Job titles included: president, senior vice president, vice president, chief medical officer, senior medical director, senior project engineer, and senior scientist. Of the sixteen participants, fourteen work in organizations with over five thousand employees; one participant owns her own consulting firm, and one is the CEO of her own accounting firm. Participants had between sixteen to thirty-two years of experience in STEM careers. All were currently employed in leadership roles with supervisory responsibilities.

Data Collection

The underlying assumption of a phenomenological study is that there are common themes within shared lived experiences that can be narrated. The goal is to understand the meaning of the phenomenon by collecting the narratives from individuals who have shared the experience (Englander 2012). Interviews elicited participants' stories, perceptions, feelings, opinions, and beliefs about their experiences with using buffering behaviors to overcome gender discrimination and provided the focal point of data collection in this study. The criterion for an effective phenomenological research interview is "as complete a description as possible of the experience the participant has lived through" (Giorgi 2009, 122). The researcher used Seidman's (2013) three-stage interview model for phenomenological inquiry. The first stage is a "focused life history" (Seidman 2013, 21) that inquires about experiences from the participant's past. The second stage focuses on the details of the participant's experiences in the present, and the third stage asks the participant to reflect on the meaning of her experiences with the phenomenon (Seidman 2013).

All but one of the interviews took place within sixty- to ninety-minute face-to-face meetings held in private offices and conference rooms selected by the participants. One interview was conducted by telephone, and both the interviewer and the interviewee were in private offices during the call. The researcher utilized a script (appendix A) that began with an explanation of the study and a request for the participant's written consent. The researcher provided a consent form to each participant, and interviewing did not begin until the participant read and signed the consent form and returned it to the researcher.

For the telephone interview, the consent form was electronically sent, signed, and returned prior to the commencement of the interview. The researcher audio-recorded all interviews with the permission of the participant. After the interviews, the researcher submitted the recordings to a professional transcription service, and the verbatim comments were returned in the form of a Word document transcript. Transcripts and MP3 digital recordings are housed in confidential computer files. Interviews ranged from fifty-six minutes to 174 minutes and averaged seventy-seven minutes per interview.

Data Analysis

The goal of data analysis in a qualitative phenomenological study is to describe as accurately as possible the common themes, the broad concepts, and the fundamental essence of a shared phenomenon by recording, coding, and analyzing the lived experiences of individuals who have personal knowledge of the phenomenon. This study incorporated Giorgi's four-step process of data analysis from his *Scientific Phenomenological Psychological Method* (2009, 128–37) and Saldaña's first cycle and second cycle coding processes (Saldaña 2012), which are described below:

Step 1: Read for a Sense of the Whole

Attribute coding provided context for the data analysis performed in step 1 by describing the setting in which the study takes place, the participant demographics and salient characteristics, the data collection format, and the time frame within which the data were collected (Saldaña 2012). The researcher first read the entire set of transcriptions to get a sense of the whole and to understand what the description is about (Giorgi 2009, 126). Prior to beginning data collection and throughout the data analysis process, the researcher conducted subjectivity audits in order to identify areas of potential subjectivity (Peshkin 1988).

Step 2: Determination of Meaning Units

In step 2 of data analysis, the researcher read each transcript in its entirety several times and began to identify recurring elements by color
coding phrases and sections (Giorgi 2009; Whiting 2002). The process of
phenomenological reduction or de-contextualizing removes units of text
from their source while keeping their meaning intact (Burnard 1994).
These segments of text are the meaning units that convey one idea, one
episode, or one piece of information (Burnard 1994; Welsch 2002).

The first cycle coding method in step 2 of data analysis used in vivo
coding, which captured the participant's actual words to create codes.
In vivo coding is particularly useful when the researcher wishes to
honor the voices of the participants (Saldaña 2012). In vivo coding ensures that the first cycle codes are generated by participant experience
rather than researcher interpretation.

As meaning units were identified, they were coded using actual words
or phrases that are descriptive of discrete elements from the participant's
lived experiences. The researcher then identified the theme that stood
out in each meaning unit and listed them (Groenewald 2004; Saldaña
2012). Originally, there were fourteen themes. The researcher initially
used the software program NVivo 7.0 to analyze the data and to assist in
classifying, sorting, and coding information. Subsequently the researcher
analyzed and organized recurring themes in the transcripts through vi-
sual inspection and by using the find function in Microsoft Word.

Step 3: Interrogating the Data and Transforming
Meaning Units into Phenomenological Expressions

This stage involved in-depth questioning of the data and asking, "What
does this tell me about women's experiences with buffering behaviors
in overcoming gender bias as they seek senior leadership positions in
male-dominated STEM?" The researcher examined both the meaning
units and the themes in light of the phenomenon. Giorgi described this

step as "interrogating each meaning unit to discover how to express in a more satisfactory way the psychological implications of the lifeworld description" (Giorgi 2009, 131). Step 3 of data analysis utilized the second cycle coding method known as pattern coding, in which overarching themes are identified and metacodes are developed (Saldaña 2012).

Step 4: Structural Synthesis

After a thorough examination of the identified phenomenological themes, the researcher composed unifying statements that tied together each of the "essential non-redundant themes" (Whiting 2002, 69). The structural synthesis stage of data analysis is presented in chapter 5 and integrates the data in order to describe the meaning and essence of the phenomenon (Creswell 2013; Moustakas 1994).

Data Classification

Three Categories of Phenomena

Three major categories of phenomena (see figure 5) emerged from this study: (a) the role of self-efficacy in the use of buffering behaviors by women leaders in STEM, (b) the gender-based barriers women encountered that required the use of buffering behaviors in STEM organizations and cultures, and (c) descriptions of the buffering behaviors that women leaders in STEM employed to advance in their ~~carriers~~ careers. The research classified data according to the conceptual frameworks that inform the phenomenological experiences of the participants. Specifically, this study examined four gender-based barriers that women most often encountered in male-dominated professions: (a) the masculine stereotype of leadership and hegemony, (b) gender bias, (c.) gender backlash, and (d.) gendered organizations. Rich descriptions of women leaders' experiences in the use of four buffering behaviors—(a) self-management, (b) impression management, (c) political skill, and (d) performance—provided a template of behaviors that successfully mitigated the impact of these gender-based barriers.

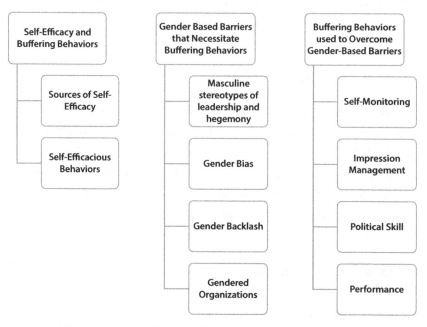

Figure 4. Three categories of major phenomena of study: (a) role of self-efficacy in buffering behaviors, (b) gender-based barriers necessitating buffering behaviors, (c) buffering behaviors utilized by STEM women to overcome gender-based barriers.

Theoretical Concepts, Major Phenomena, and Themes

The themes that emerged in each of the three major categories of phenomena—the role of self-efficacy in the use of buffering behaviors by women leaders in STEM, the gender-based barriers women leaders in STEM encountered that required the use of buffering behaviors, and the buffering behaviors that women leaders in STEM employed to advance in their careers—will be presented in the following sections.

Category 1: Unifying Theory of Self-Efficacy

The first major category of phenomena, the unifying theory of the role of self-efficacy, produced two subcategories: Sources of self-efficacy and the role of self-efficacy in buffering behaviors. Each of the two subcategories produced two themes. The two themes under the sub-category of sources of self-efficacy are: theme 1: early messages and experiences, and theme 2: athletic experiences and/or physical challenges. The themes under the subcategory role of self-efficacy in buffering behaviors are: theme 4: positive self-talk, and theme 5: taking control of one's career destiny (See figure 6).

Self-efficacy proved to be an essential ingredient in women's ability to confront and surmount the gender-based barriers they encountered in STEM. The sources of self-efficacy and the use of self-efficacious behaviors provided important data regarding the success strategies of women leaders in STEM.

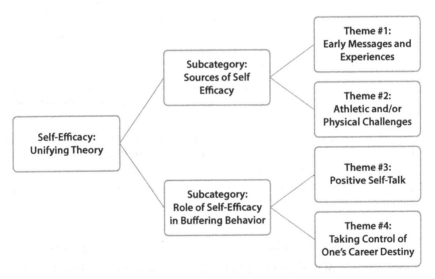

Figure 5. Diagram showing the two subcategories and four themes within the unifying theory of self-efficacy.

Category 2: Gender-Based Barriers

Four categories of gender-based barriers, (a) masculine stereotypes of leadership and hegemony, (b) gender bias, (c) gender backlash, and (d) gendered organizations yielded four themes. The four themes include: theme 5: STEM is a man's world—power will not be shared nor given to women, theme 6: a prevailing belief that women cannot and will not perform well in STEM, theme 7: you will not last—we will freeze you out, and theme 8: you don't belong here—you are not welcome here.

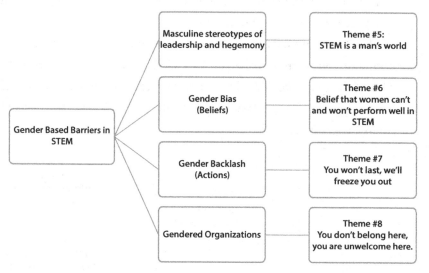

Figure 6. Diagram showing the conceptual framework the gender-based barriers most often encountered by women seeking leaderhship in STEM. The barriers include masculine stereotypes of leadership and male hegemony, gender bias, gender backlash, and gendered organizations. and produced four themes.

The gender-based barriers identified in figure 7 gave rise to the development of the buffering behaviors that women employed to overcome these barriers.

Category 3: Buffering Behaviors

Recent studies have shown that there are behaviors and approaches that may attenuate negative reactions against women who exhibit counterstereotypical behavior (Gupta 2013; Moss-Racusin & Rudman 2010; O'Neill & O'Reilly 2011; Shaughnessy, Treadway, Breland, Williams, & Brouer 2011). These mitigating behaviors are referred to as buffering behaviors (O'Neill & O'Reilly 2011) and were the central focus of this study.

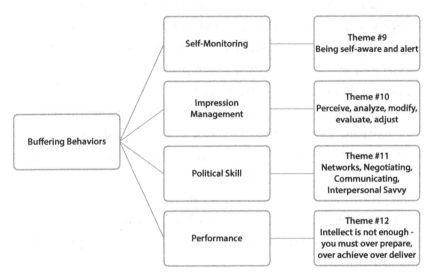

Figure 7. Chart showing the four buffering behaviors studied and the resulting four themes identified from the data.

Specific examples of buffering behaviors generated four themes and were grouped under the main theoretical subcategories of (a) self-monitoring, (b) impression management, (c) political skill, and (d) performance. The four themes included: theme 9: be self-aware and alert; theme 10: perceive, analyze, modify, evaluate, adjust; theme 11: networks, negotiating, communicating, interpersonal "savvy"; and theme 12: intellect is not enough—overprepare, overachieve, and overdeliver.

While the literature provided the theoretical frameworks that formed the infrastructure of this study, the literature lacked specific examples of how buffering behaviors have proven effective in the male-dominated STEM professions. This study fills that gap by providing illustrative examples that deepen the understanding of each theoretical concept by sharing in vivo descriptions of the concept as they are experienced in the lives of STEM women leaders. The differentiating element of this study is the focus on women who have empowered themselves to seek and to find strategies and behaviors that enabled them to surmount the gender-based obstacles they encountered and reach senior leadership positions in STEM. Detailed accounts that incorporate extensive layers of situational facts as well as the feelings, impressions, perceptions, thoughts, and reactions of the participants are provided to ensure rich, thick descriptions. Rich descriptions of women leaders' experiences in the use of buffering behaviors—self-management, impression management, political skill, and performance—provided a template of behaviors that successfully mitigated the impact of these gender-based barriers. It is through this level of descriptiveness that the reader will determine if transferability of findings is possible.

Presentation of Data and Major Themes

Themes Emerging from Central Organizing Theory: Self-Efficacy

Participants discussed the influences in their lives that helped to shape the belief systems (self-efficacy) and behavior systems (self-regulation) that enabled them to employ buffering behaviors when confronting obstacles and mistreatment related to gender. These influences included early messages from significant people in their lives, early experiences both athletic and academic, the use of positive self-talk, and the belief that they could shape their own career destiny by their decisions and actions. For a chart of the twelve themes discussed below, please see figure 8.

Phenomenon #1 Self-Efficacy	Phenomenon #2 Gender Based Barriers	Phenomenon #3 Buffering Behaviors
Theme 1: Early messages and experiences	Theme 5: STEM is a man's world – power will not be shared not given to women	Theme 9: Be self-aware and alert
Theme 2: Athletic experiences and/or physical challenges	Theme 6: A prevailing belief that women can't and won't perform well in STEM	Theme 10: Perceive, analyze, modify, evaluate, adjust
Theme 3: Positive self-talk	Theme 7: You won't last- we'll freeze you out	Theme 11: Networks, negotiating, communicating, and interpersonal savvy
Theme 4: Taking control of one's career destiny	Theme 8: You don't belong here—you are note welcome here.	Theme 12: Intellect is not enough – over-prepare, over-Achieve, and over-deliver.

Figure 8. The major themes and categories identified in this study.

Theme 1: early messages and experiences shape self-efficacy—"You did this; you can do anything." Early validating messages of competence and early experiences of being given responsibility for duties and decisions beyond what might be expected of a child were cited as influential in forming beliefs of self-efficacy among the participants. The following quotations give specific examples of how parents and teachers provided influential messages and experiences that led to the development of self-efficacy among the women in this study.

Mary: All the role models in my life said something to the
                   effect, "You can do whatever you want to do. It's up
                   to you to decide what you want to do and make it
                   happen." In one way, shape, or form, I got that mes-
                   sage very early and consistently. So I had no reason
                   to believe I couldn't.

Dale: I applied for an internship at NASA and was sched-
                   uled for an interview. I remember that day because
                   my dad drove me, and before I went into the in-
                   terview, he said, "Just remember, you can do any-
                   thing." We struggled financially, as a child. But
                   knowing that my parents had that kind of belief in
                   me was absolutely tremendous. It definitely gave me
                   a lot of self-confidence.

Randi: At home, it was always very technical-task-
                   achievement oriented. It started for me in early
                   childhood. Back in the '70s, my dad had a TRS-80,
                   and he used to say, "Randi, instead of watching car-
                   toons Saturday morning, why don't you go down-
                   stairs and write a program on the TRS-80." So I had
                   a lot of this technical input into my life from a very
                   early age. As a result, I derived a sense of accom-
                   plishment and the knowledge that I could achieve
                   almost any technical task presented. I guess that's
                   really where I get my sense of accomplishment.
                   That's really my sense of self.

Self-efficacy has been shown to be strengthened in children who
have opportunities to confront difficulties, to persist, and to overcome
them (Pajares & Schunk 2001). Gina, Yasmin, and Susan cited early
childhood experiences of responsibility that helped to imbue them with
a sense of self-efficacy.

Gina: I had a lot of adult responsibilities as a child. My parents were both from Italy … immigrants, but professional immigrants. My mother had bipolar disease, and she was not terribly functional. My brother was eight years younger than me, so I was taking care of him. So a lot of responsibility was put on me to take care of my brother, and to take care of the household, and to deal with a lot of adult issues. At a young age, I was sent on very adult missions. My mother's mother, who was already a little bit senile at the time, decided she wanted to go to Italy to reclaim her prewar apartment in Florence, and I had to accompany her and go to lawyers and handle this. I had a lot of adult responsibilities as a teenager.

Yasmin: My mom had an accident when I was very young, so since I was eight or nine I was always very responsible, I had to be. I had to grow up very fast, and I was always my mom's right hand. So that, of course, creates a belief in you that you can do it; I can do this.

Susan: It might actually be the struggle. There is a Persian proverb that says the eagle can only rise if the wind is against it—that the wind that's against you can actually provide uplift. And when you're in a bad situation, it might not be that comfortable, but, in retrospect, if I hadn't had that obstacle, it would have been hard for me to grow through the experience and to learn.

Theme 2: athletic and/or physical challenges—you learn to compete, confront obstacles, and achieve goals. Participants in this study described the importance of competitive sports and physical challenges such as those encountered in Outward Bound programs in developing self-efficacy. Five of the women in the study reported that early experiences in sports or physical challenges contributed to feelings of self-efficacy.

Gina: Athletics provided a feeling of control. I think it may be that if you are able to control your body in some way, that you have control of your mind and a lot of other things. It's sort of tangible—if you can run a mile then you can run a race—it's a feeling of control.

Claire: I loved sports as a kid. It responds to effort. You understand what the scales are, what the measures are—it's much simpler than real life. So you can practice being confident and working at something and training and practicing and getting good at something. A sports environment is where you can work on teams and be leaders in teams. I became very comfortable in my skin through sports, really.

I have two daughters. Everything's embarrassing from the age of about eleven. Your self-confidence takes a hit too because you want to be beautiful. You want to belong. It's a very powerful and vulnerable period from the age of ten or eleven through about sixteen, seventeen. I think I was able to put aside all of that static by just enjoying the simplicity of sports. I think my younger daughter got through it with Outward Bound. She captained a boat and during a period of bad weather, took charge because she realized it needed to be done. She just did it, and said, "Wow, I did this thing." From that day forward, she was able to do anything she set her mind to. It was an incredible transformation. So I think it's important for girls and young women to have some kind of challenge that they step up and take on. And then you know that in your bones that you can do that.

Theme 3: positive self-talk—"I know I can do this—this is where I belong." Self–talk is a conscious and cognitive activity that incorporates both motivating and instructional statements although motivational statements have shown to have greater positive impact on enhancing performance and limiting critical thoughts (Hatzigeorgiadis 2006). The following comments by Alice, Randi, Tess, and Amy demonstrate the cognitive activity of self-talk and its role in their self-efficacious behavior.

Alice: Each time I've started something, I've thought, *Oh God, how do I compete with these brains around the table?* But I have this mantra that I say to myself if I'm thinking, *Oh, maybe I can't do it. Maybe I can't do it."* I think, *Remember you were top of your class in medical school,* which I was, number one, *you were top of your class at Harvard. You didn't dream that. You didn't imagine that. You can do this.*

Randi: When people doubt me, I think, *That doesn't really matter because I know I can do this. I know I'm capable of this. This is my thing. This is where I belong.*

Tess: If you grew up in a Catholic environment, you were told, "If you don't use your talents, it's a sin." I felt my talent was being smart; that was the talent given to me. In fifth grade, I decided I was going to be a physician, a pediatrician. I told myself, *Well, medicine is hard, so no one could accuse me of not using my talents if I went into medicine.* And that's what I did.

Amy: My influence was from my father. His most famous piece of advice was, "Life is not fair. Whoever said it was meant to be?" So when my boss said, "Hey, you're a woman. You don't belong out there in the field." I thought, *Well okay, that's not too fair.* So when something that wasn't fair was happening, I was able to accept it, and figure out how to be a little subversive.

Alice: When I think of the guys that I was in med school with who were not as bright or as able as I was, ... I think, "I'll be damned if I'm going to let him be my boss." I think that kind of pushes me forward. I think, "You know what? If they can do it, I can do it." That's always the thing that pushes me on, you know, my inner feminist.

Dale: I definitely think my intellect has been very helpful. When I'm in a situation where I have doubt, I always say to myself, *You have the ability to figure this out. You weren't given this IQ not to do anything with it. Just calm down, use the brain that you were given, and you can solve this.*

Theme 4: "Take control of your career and destiny." Self-efficacy was instrumental in the participants' persistence in the face of obstacles, proactive problem solving when discriminatory selection methods or gender-based pay discrepancies were discovered, to volunteer for difficult assignments, to take control of their own career paths, and to leave untenable situations. The following examples illustrate how the self-percepts of efficacy were instrumental in the courses of actions that women chose.

Jennifer: You have to be in control of your own destiny and know what you want. I was interviewing a woman, and she wanted me to help her define her career. She asked, "Should I go into the public sector? Should I go into consulting? I don't know what I want." I told her you have to know what you want and then go for it. You can't expect others to guide you. That's probably more difficult for women to maneuver in a male-dominated profession, but that's the advice I give.

Yasmin: When I realized that I was doing more work, being paid less, and not being promoted at the same rate as my male peers, I put all the facts on the table, and I said, "Okay, this is what's happening. I have been here for x amount of years, this is what I'm doing— this is what I've done." And the funny thing was that my boss knew exactly what was happening. I said, "You knew and you're not doing anything?" He said, "Well, we didn't know that you wanted to do more." And at that moment, my career, my life, took a turn. If you don't take control of your life, you don't get opportunities, and it's not because people don't want to give them to you, it's because they don't know you want them. You have to ask.

Randi: I used to think that if I did a good job I'd get noticed. But you can get stuck doing that. You can't hang back and wait to be noticed. It's not enough to do a good job. You have to look for opportunities and raise your hand and say, "I want to do that," and then hope somebody will give you the chance.

When participants in the study discovered gender-based pay inequity, or realized they were in situations that were untenable, they behaved self-efficaciously and proactively sought remedy, or they left the organization to pursue other opportunities. Claire, Tess, Gina, Randi, and Karen all gave examples of self-efficaciously taking their careers into their own hands.

Claire: There was one point in my career where I had two men reporting to me, and they were both making substantially more money than I was. For a while,

I thought, *Okay, that's the way it is. They're technical experts, so they deserve to be highly compensated.* But then I realized, *No, that's not right. I'm just as technically knowledgeable as they are. I have the same years of experience. I'm working on bigger projects, and I'm bringing in more business, and they report to me.* When I pointed it out to my supervisor, he said, "Oh. We just kind of thought that was normal." But when I said, "I don't think this is right," he looked at it and said, "Well, yeah. We should do something about that." But it hadn't occurred to him. If I had waited for him to come to that conclusion, it never would have happened. So you have to step up.

Tess: When I discovered that my male colleagues were being paid substantially more than me, and I realized that I've invested fifteen years in my medical training, I decided I'm worth more than that. A colleague said, "Why don't you think about going into industry?" She told me about a local company that recruited physicians who had basic science and clinical training. And I said, "You know what, it's another risk. I came to this country, and that was a risk. I went to Harvard for my postdoc, and that was a risk. So why not roll the dice and take another risk?

Gina   When I was trying to do innovative things and challenge the status quo, I was pretty much shut out by the male physicians. I started to doubt whether I wanted to continue practicing medicine because I felt like I couldn't practice good medicine in the context that I was in. I met a nurse who was working in a pharmaceutical company, and I asked her, "Do they ever hire physicians?" She said, "As a matter of fact, they're looking for someone to head up my department. Are you interested?" The following week I had an interview. At the end of the interview, they offered me the job, and I thought, *You know what, I'm going to go for it.*

Karen: When the founding partners (my dad was one) turned the firm over to the second generation, they let it go stagnant. I didn't like what the second generation was doing. I was networking. I had the most billable hours and the most clients. So five of us women decided to leave—we broke off and left the firm. That was a hard thing to do. I left the firm that my father founded. And my dad and I were pretty close.

Bandura's social cognitive theory (2001) suggests that self-efficacy may be central to the ability of some women to successfully enter challenging situations, be persistent, and achieve long-held goals. Alice, Ann, and Karen offered examples of perseverance in the face of obstacles illustrating the essential role of self-efficacy when confronting gender-based barriers.

Alice: My chair was blocking me from accepting research opportunities and from defending my thesis so he could keep me in his department doing his work. I thought, *Okay. I'm not going to take it. I'm going to take this further.* So I went to a neurologist in another department. I had built credibility with him. He was very measured, and said, "You have to make it difficult for him to stop you. Go back to your office, schedule your thesis defense, put it on his calendar. Say, 'I am defending. I am graduating this year.' Demonstrate determination." I did it; it worked. I learned to take action when a situation is untenable.

Ann: A woman in medical school had not done well on her oral boards, and our chairman came storming into the residents' room, and in a loud voice said to me, "I just found out that so and so flunked her boards. Are you going flunk your boards too?" I was furious. I thought that was completely unfair. The only link between me and the other person was gender. I said, "Not if you do your job and teach me." I ended up thinking it was better to confront these things and not let them pass, to stand up against them, and it actually did toughen me up and prepare me for handling situations that I would move into after I finished training. I decided I can't let him walk on me.

Karen: We had a couple of male clients that were very difficult. I'd say we just need to terminate them, which is highly unusual to do in the accounting world—to terminate a client. But I'm the type that believes it's not worth always having somebody treat you that way. It's just not worth it. It's worked very well when I've said, "I've had it. I'm not going to work with you." They backed down.

Themes Emerging from Gender-Based Barriers in STEM

Every woman in the study reported experiencing gender-based discriminatory behaviors, beliefs, decisions, and actions, and that it caught them by surprise. These experiences ranged from caustic, degrading, and demeaning remarks to exclusion from work-related social activities to an actual sexual assault by an attending physician upon one of the women when she was a medical student. Participants gave examples of gender-based barriers in the form of pay differentials for the same work, the role of the good old boy club in promotions, and exclusion from career-enhancing networks.

Theme 5: "STEM is a man's world—power will not be shared nor given to women." The literature offers evidence of numerous gender-based barriers that have their origin in masculine stereotypes of leadership and masculine hegemony. An important aspect for consideration when examining the masculine stereotype of leadership is the concept of masculine hegemony, or "the maintenance of practices that allowed men's dominance over women to continue" (Connell & Messerschmidt 2005, 832).

Women reported episodes of hazing and mistreatment at the hands of male supervisors who did not want them in the organization. They also found that their male peers and colleagues would watch silently and not speak up to challenge inappropriate behavior. Many women reported incidents when they felt they were alone in the battle to achieve their career aspirations.

Jennifer: It was tough. There were a bunch of guys working for me who wanted the job I got. There didn't think I deserved the job. All they did was tell me how I should do my job, but they would not help. When I put stuff on their plate, they threw it back at me … It was a hard dynamic because not only was I a woman, I was probably the youngest person at this job level at the time. These guys were close to retirement and had been doing this job forever. They didn't want to be told what to do.

Claire: Our team had several scientific papers accepted, so a group of us went to the conference to present them. I was the only woman. We were encouraged to put reprints of our papers out in the booth and to put our business cards next to our papers. I put all of my business cards out and went into a session. When I came back, I found that somebody had taken all of my business cards and written, "Girl Engineer", under my name on every single business card. It was our boss who had done that. He thought it was funny. But clearly, he was hazing me. He was telling me that "you're here, but you don't belong here." All

of the men who came along on that trip knew it was
him, knew he'd done it. They were very uncomfort-
able, but nobody said anything. Nobody was willing
to challenge the big man about this thing that he'd
done.

Sabine described an experience that was similar to those reported
by other participants in which male colleagues witnessed inappropriate
and demeaning behavior but stood by silently and did not intervene,
thereby enabling masculine hegemonic behavior to persist.

Sabine: I was scheduled to make a proposal to the head of
                   our division, and I was very well prepared. However,
                   when I entered the meeting room to make my pre-
                   sentation, the division head started talking about
                   the heavy drinking he and the other men in the
                   meeting had done the night before and about the
                   women they met in the bar. It made me incredi-
                   bly uncomfortable, and it became clear that he was
                   not going to listen to a word that came out of my
                   mouth. I felt it was because I was the only female
                   on the team, and he made it clear he didn't think I
                   belonged there. I guess, for me the saddest part of
                   that situation was that I knew everybody else in that
                   room didn't feel that way, but they didn't have the
                   balls to stand up to him.

Sexual harassment, a subset of masculine hegemony. All sixteen
of the study participants reported experiencing gender-based discriminatory practices and forms of sexual harassment either during their
academic preparation or in the workplace. Sexual harassment in medical training is common with 73 percent of female residents reporting
incidents of sexual harassment and that the harassers are most often attending physicians or medical faculty (Komaromy, Bindman, Haber, &
Sande 1993). Ann, Sabine, Gina, and Amy all recounted similar incidents

of sexual harassment that occurred in their university or medical school years and early in their careers.

Ann:

In my first year of medical school, there were lecturers who tried to keep the attention level high by sprinkling in all kinds of crude jokes, slides of nude women, all kinds of things. And I have to say that I was shocked. I was appalled. I found it distracting; I found it annoying, and I just didn't know emotionally how to deal with it. I thought, *What's going on here? I've never seen anything like this before.* In small groups, it would be the same thing. Your gender was being held up as something for ridicule.

Sabine:

In my first year after engineering school, I spent most of my time in the field, interacting with blue collar drillers. That was the highest level of misogyny that I experienced in my career. There were definitely men that had conversations with my chest instead of my face.

Amy:

There were experiences that were unique to women. The first time I experienced it was in graduate school. The head of the civil engineering department was a big, powerful guy. And he would trap me up against the wall. I always had to fend him off, but you were aware that the guys didn't have to deal with that. It was a stress. Graduate school is already filled with plenty of stress. I'm not confrontational. I was always plotting how to get away. But I also recognized the power that he had. You had to figure that out. You didn't want him to get mad. I can still remember him pinning me up against the wall and saying "Come into my office." I wondered why was that happening to me? I realized it was because I was the only girl.

Gina:	In medical school I was a stellar intern. The person who supervises you is called the attending physician. My rotation was over, and I hadn't gotten my grade yet, but it was scheduled to come out the next week. One day, my doorbell rang, and there is the attending physician at my door, which really shocked me. He was a middle-aged, balding, overweight guy. He was not a welcome sight, and I was a little startled. I let him come into my apartment, and then he physically attacked me; he tried to, essentially, get me to have sex with him. And I knew at that moment that my career was at stake because he had all the power. I had nothing, and knew that I had to make a decision at that moment. Do I go with this, or do I kick him out? I kicked him out. Then my grade came in, and it was a B, which was not good enough for the competitive programs. So, I couldn't apply to the strong academic centers. I thought, *These guys own the world.*
Amy:	It must've been my second year at the firm, and one evening around 5:00 p.m.—those were the days where at 5:00 p.m., all the vice presidents had refrigerators, and the whiskey bottles used to come out and the cups. So, it was not unusual that at 5:00 p.m., my boss already had been drinking. He came and sat on my desk and said, "You need to come to my office." He was three sheets to the wind and said all these inappropriate things. He said, "I wanna know you. We need to go out." I was mortified. Somehow, I escaped. But the next day, I didn't know what to do.

Theme 6: "Women can't and won't perform well in STEM."
Gender bias is the antipathy directed toward women who seek positions of power that men traditionally hold (Glick & Fiske 2001). In studies on formal and informal forms of gender bias and discrimination, one of

the most common obstacles reported by women was "an inhospitable corporate culture (Weele & Heilman 2005, 31). Amy, Jennifer, Nathalie, Randi, Mary, and Tess gave examples of how gender bias was expressed toward them and how discouraging these experiences were.

Amy: One day my boss came to me and said, "I'm going to send you out in the field with the field group. We've got fifty wells that need to be sampled." I thought that was the most exciting thing in the world. I said, "Great." Then I got a visit from my boss's boss. He came into my cube and said, "I just need you to know that the field is no place for women. You can do what you want, but I just need to let you know what my opinion is. I need you to know that." I just looked at him. I don't think I said anything. I was thirty years old. What would you say?

Jennifer: So, being the radical person that I was in the '70s or the early '80s, I had one of those buttons on my jacket that said $0.67, which was a women's salary compared to a man's salary. My engineering professor looked at it and then gave me a look, sneered, and said, "Go back to the kitchen where you belong." Seriously. I am not kidding. I remember just feeling this pit in my stomach and thinking, *Oh my god, is this what I'm going to encounter in engineering?* I didn't respond. It still sticks with me to this day and I have told and retold this story a number of times to people because it was something that I didn't expect from a professor.

Ann: After a conference, we all piled into a car to go to dinner, and our chairman and mentor remarked to the resident sitting beside him, "I don't think there's any place in medicine for women." I couldn't believe it. I thought, *Oh, my gosh, I'm in this program who's*

*run by a guy who thinks there's no place in medicine for
women.*

Randi: I went to my adviser, who had recommended me for
                    the five-year master's program, and I said to him, "I
                    have this job opportunity. It's exciting." And he said,
                    "Well, I suppose it doesn't really matter if you get
                    your master's or not because you're just gonna be a
                    housewife in a few years anyway." That was such a
                    slap in the face because my goals were never to be
                    home taking care of the kids and the house. Never.

Mary: One of my engineering professors told a woman in
                    our class that he didn't know why she was bothering
                    to go to college anyways because didn't women just
                    go to engineering school to find a husband?

Claire: Early on, I asked my boss for career advice, and he
                    just said to me flatly, "You should be at home with
                    your children." Yeah. He said, "You should be at
                    home with your children. You shouldn't be here."
                    That was my career advice.

**Theme 7: "You won't last. We'll freeze you out. You will be
ill treated for violating gender stereotypes."** The third conceptual
element of the study encompasses a double bind that aspiring women
often face known as gender backlash (Garcia-Retamero & Lopez-Zafra
2006; Heilman, Wallen, Fuchs, & Tamkins 2004; O'Neill & O'Reilly
2011). Gender backlash is defined as "social and economic sanctions
for counterstereotypical behavior" (Rudman & Fairchild 2004, 157;
Rudman, Moss-Racusin, Phelan, & Nauts 2012, 166).

Ann, Sabine, Susan, and Kate reported that the attainment of senior leadership positions resulted in a backlash reaction from male
colleagues.

Ann:

When I was selected to be chair of the department, a colleague told me that one of the department heads said, "Have you heard Ann was chosen? She won't last. We'll freeze her out." And that was exactly the way I felt when I walked into my first executive meeting with all the other chairs. Not a person said hello to me, not a single person. It was like walking into a freezer, into an ice storage space. I remember listening at that first meeting and thinking, *I'll see how these things go.* I found the same thing that I had seen as a faculty member—tons of bombastic comments being made; whoever spoke loudest, whoever had the biggest department, whoever had the most money, their opinion was what counted. I remember trying to speak at one of the meetings, and my dean said, "I want to hear what someone else has to say." I can still see his hand going up to stop me. I never did get to speak.

Sabine:

In some cases, no matter what I said, I was going to get push back because when you are a female authority figure, people project upon you all of the other horrible female authority figures that they have had to deal with, and sometimes you have to take the brunt of that.

Susan:

Take a man and woman starting the same new job—the man talks about his new assignment as if he's done this for a long time and knows it all, and it's perceived quite well. The woman does exactly the same thing, the reaction you hear is, "Did you hear that? She doesn't know what she's talking about. It's complete nonsense." And I've seen that happen in the hospital, as well as in this research environment, and it's fascinating because it really does bring back this concept of the boys club. It's sort of, "Oh,

yeah, he's one of us," and the backslaps, and all that.
Women just don't fit in like that.

Kate: There's a senior woman in the firm who is super in-
                      sightful, has a great head for business, and is a great
                      problem solver. But she tells it like it is. She doesn't
                      hold back. So if a project isn't going well, she tells
                      everybody what they're doing wrong. When some
                      senior people were messing up and making poor
                      decisions, she told them very directly. It has hurt her
                      career. Even though there are men who do exactly
                      the same thing, and are admired for being straight
                      shooters, she can't be a straight shooter because they
                      don't want to be told by a woman when they've
                      messed up.

Theme 8: "You don't belong here; you are unwelcome here."
STEM organizations are highly gendered, and the cultural climate
has often been reported as inhospitable to women (Acker 2006; Fox
& Colatrella 2006; Lemons & Parzinger 2001; Von Hellens, Nielsen,
& Trauth 2001; Wentling & Thomas 2009). Descriptions of STEM or-
ganizations and cultures include phrases such as, "largely white, male
dominated, anti-social, individualistic, and competitive" (Wentling &
Thomas 2009, 27).

All sixteen participants in this study recounted experiences that
illustrated the inequality regimes based on gender schema that are
prevalent in STEM organizations. Tess, Karen, Jennifer, Gina, Claire,
and Amy described incidents in which men were invited to participate
in social activities that established relationships that proved to be helpful when seeking career advancement but from which women were
excluded. These activities often created career opportunities.

Tess: In medical school, when you are deciding on your
                      area of specialty, the physicians would say to some

of the students, "Why don't we go out golfing?" And they'd invite the male students or interns or residents; they wouldn't think to invite the female students and residents. And sometimes it's those connections that help you get that plum residency or that position or that influence.

Karen: The senior partner of the firm would take the guys out drinking, golfing. He'd always invite them out to do what little bit of networking that he did do— what he considered networking. He always took the guys.

Interviewer: And you were not invited?

Karen: Oh, no, no, no, never.

Jennifer: There was this golf league that they had where the guys go out and play golf on Wednesday nights. I said, "Hey, can I join you? I like to play golf (and I'm pretty good, but I didn't say that)," and they said, "This is the royal and ancient men's golf league. We don't allow women to play."

Vivian and Gina described the gendered organization as a "men's club" from which women are excluded and in which career decisions are often made.

Vivian: There is a middle-aged white man club; if you're a woman, you cannot be part of that, and that prevents you from moving up. I've seen it way too often ... a promotion that is not based on knowledge or results, but social connection because the upper management is mainly men. If you want to go out and take a drink with a man, you can't do it as a woman, right? It would be viewed as inappropriate,

whereas if I'm a man, I can always invite my buddy
and say, "Hey, let's have a drink," and that's okay.

Gina   Well, it's a club. And you want a club that you
            can feel comfortable just relaxing in. If you have
            women around, you can't let your hair down. It's the
            Mitt Romney issue; it's the binders full of women.
            Everybody's got binders full of women, and that's
            where they stay—on the shelf.

Karen and Gina described situations in which they were denied
equal access to career opportunities based on their gender.

Gina: I recall one interview for medical school where the
            interviewer asked me, "Why should we waste a
            space on a woman who is never going to practice?"
            I said, "Well, I do intend to practice. But even if I
            were to take five years off to raise a family, given
            the differential longevity of women and the prema-
            ture atherosclerosis in men, my total practice years
            would probably exceed that of my male counter-
            parts." I didn't get into that medical school.

Karen: When we were starting our own accounting firm,
            we went to the bank to arrange financing. The
            banker said, "I think you can qualify for an SBA loan
            because you're female—a minority firm." But they
            wanted our husbands to sign the loan. I said, "My
            husband doesn't know jack diddly about accounting.
            Why should he be on the hook for an accounting
            firm that he's not going have anything to do with?"
            But we couldn't get the SBA loan without our hus-
            bands signing. That was very frustrating.

Evidence of gender-based discriminatory barriers in STEM is extensive and inequality regimes appear to be widespread. The participants

in this study recount an array of mitigating behaviors that they employed to overcome these barriers. These buffering behaviors are the central focus of this study and are described in the next section.

Themes Emerging from Buffering Behaviors

The first four elements of the conceptual framework describe the organizational challenges confronting many women and include (a) the generally held belief that leadership is a masculine domain, (b) the gender stereotypes that lead to bias, (c) gender backlash women encounter when they behave counterstereotypically, and (d) the gendered culture of many STEM organizations. Yet, there are women who persist, persevere, and succeed in reaching senior levels of leadership in STEM professions.

Recent studies have shown that certain buffering behaviors enable many self-efficacious women to overcome the gender-based challenges they often encounter as they seek to attain senior leadership roles in STEM organizations (Cech, Rubineau, Silbey, & Seron 2011; Gupta 2013; Jalbert, Jalbert, & Furumo 2013; O'Neill & O'Reilly 2011; Shaughnessy et al. 2011; Todd, Harris, Harris, & Wheeler 2009). These buffering behaviors include, but are not limited to, self-monitoring (Bandura 2001; Gupta 2013; O'Neill & O'Reilly 2011) impression management (Hirshfield 2011; O'Neill & O'Reilly 2011; Singh, Kumra, & Vinnicombe 2002), political skill (Shaughnessy, Treadway, Breland, Williams, & Brouer 2011; Todd, Harris, Harris, & Wheeler 2009), and performance (Jalbert, Jalbert, & Furumo 2013). The following section provides rich and thick descriptions of buffering behaviors in the areas of self-monitoring, impression management, political skill, and performance. The data on buffering behaviors produced four themes.

Self-monitoring. Theme 9: be alert and self-aware. Self-monitoring is a behavioral technique in which people assess and adjust their behavior within interpersonal and organizational situations and appears to be an effective buffering strategy for overcoming gender bias and backlash (Flynn & Ames 2006; Rudman & Phelan 2008; Shivers-Blackwell 2006). People who self-monitor closely observe social cues and use this information to guide their behavior, which is particularly helpful to women in organizations where strong gender norms exist (O'Neill & O'Reilly 2011). The women in this study all reported an awareness of self-monitoring and a heightened consciousness of both behaviors and language that might set them apart in a negative way.

Yasmin: You always have to be alert; you must be careful how you express yourself. Even in your day-to-day work. you know, a silly comment that should be taken as a joke is fine if it is made by a male co-worker, but if it's made by a woman, they will say "she doesn't know what's she's talking about."

Alice: I feel like I have so many things working against me. I'm a foreign medical graduate. I'm working outside of my specialty. I'm a woman. I'm also a very young woman. I have to try even harder than other people because I feel like I have these "dings." I don't have an inferiority complex, but I feel like you have to have that insight in order to be able to balance it through behaviors and things that you do. It's part of every single meeting, everything I do. Every time I walk into a room, I'm aware of, "Who's sitting where at the table?" It's something you have to be aware of every day: what you wear to work, how you present—you have to engineer this thing.

Randi: One of my concerns is my tendency to listen and then say, "Okay, so what you're saying is ...," and "Let's think about how we can accomplish that." I'm afraid it makes me sound like I am giving in to their position or am unwilling to stick to my guns. I think that the stereotype of women is that they tend to be less forceful and defer a lot. But I believe that if you work with me long enough, you understand that what I'm trying to do is reach a reasonable position between what I'm thinking and what you're thinking. So we've got to talk to each other and work it out, but I don't want to seem deferential. I don't want to seem like I am just doing what someone else recommends because they said so. It's a dilemma.

Susan: There's a fine balance between appearing confident and being perceived as overconfident. It's very tricky. In fact, it's extremely tricky, and it seems to be, almost, walking on a tightrope, but you can't feel it, and you can't see it.

Ann: After we circulated the petition asking that the professors stop using lewd pictures of women in our lectures, one of the women in the class was called into the dean's office and was told, "Do not associate with those troublemakers." That's when I knew that I had to stay quiet and could not rock the boat. I needed to try to find that path that everyone else was taking, but I didn't know what it was. I remember being on rounds and not feeling as prepared as I would like. How do you behave on rounds? How do you deliver a good report? I was never given any instruction or advice, and I always suspected that some of the guys had been told how they were supposed to make their presentations, etc. I really had to just observe, try to pick it up because it wasn't coming directly in the form of mentorship or anything like that.

Amy: I think I alternated along the way from not rocking the boat to confronting things. And I think I learned to assess the environment that I was in and decide what was the best approach.

Yasmin: You always have to be alert; you have to be careful
               in how you express yourself. You have to make sure
               you know your audience. You have to dress and
               project yourself the way you want them to see you.
               If you don't do that, if you don't present yourself that
               way, I don't care how smart you are, it's going to be
               hard. You need to make sure people see a person
               that is very confident.

Kate   Yeah, I'm much more calm on the outside. The in-
               side may be nerve wracked, but I won't let it show—
               no, because that just shows vulnerability.

**Impression management. Theme 10: "Analyze, evaluate, adjust
your behaviors."** The first buffering behavior, self-monitoring, provides a framework within which individuals formulate new behaviors
and actions in order to create positive public impressions. Those who
actively self-monitor are more likely to utilize the buffering behavior
of impression management (Gangestad & Snyder 2000).

Impression management, also known as self-presentation, is a conscious process by which individuals seek to create a specific impression
on others to elicit certain reactions (Guadagno & Cialdini 2007; Singh,
Kumra, & Vinnicombe 2002). The data show that the study participants
are constantly aware of specific behavior choices such as appearance,
semantics, group affiliations, and meeting behavior. Five behavioral
subsets of impression management emerged from the data: (a) executive
appearance, (b) communication and language choices, (c) associations,
(d) adapting and adjusting, and (e) differentiating yourself.

Impression management: executive appearance.

Kate: I'm thoughtful about what I wear. I'll think about
               what earrings I put on, how much perfume, is the
               hair right, what shoes what do you feel comfortable
               in? You're thoughtful about where you sit, what you

bring with you, how you handle yourself when you sit down, when you pipe up, who you connect with at the table, who you make eye contact with.

Sabine: What I try to do is always be appropriate for the situation and use the way I look to my advantage given the audience that I know I'm going to have. I will admit that I have used my height and stature in ways to assert myself. You need to use the tools that you have. The more important the meeting, the higher the heels. I try to make myself a presence.

Randi: It's so hard to know what being a woman has to do with my behavior. I think that I do try to make sure that I'm consciously making decisions to keep that off the table. For instance, I actually hired someone to help me with my wardrobe because at some point, you move from being a back-office programmer to meeting with people. She worked with me on how to put together outfits, how to present myself in a professional manner, and also did some shopping with me. I almost never have my fingernails painted. And that's because you don't want to be presented as someone who's frivolous, not that having your nails done is frivolity, but it can be perceived that way. You don't want to be perceived as being fussy at all—you want to be perceived as very down to earth. "We're getting stuff done. We're focused on the task and the subject matter at hand."

Karen: I make it a point to either wear red or hot pink, which is a power color. I like to be out there and do that.

Dale: I always try to look like I belong to the part. I do think it helps others respect you more. When I started my career, I was in total denial. I was like,

"I'm going to achieve this, and I'm not going to
wear a suit for it." I had totally the wrong attitude.
Because it felt like I was giving in to a norm. Now, I
always wear a suit.

Impression management researchers point out that the use of impression management is not necessarily intended to project a false
persona but is, instead, a mechanism for overcoming inaccurate stereotypical perceptions (Leary & Kowalski 1990). Yasmin emphasized this
fact in the following comment:

Yasmin: So you must be aware of the audience and who's
               around you. That's how you know how you're going
               to present yourself or communicate or react or stand
               or sit. But that doesn't mean you're going to become
               a different person. I want to make that clear. You're
               still you; it's me; I'm the same person. It's hard to
               explain, but you need to know that, and I think you
               have to apply that to many different situations.

Impression management: communication and language choices.
Participants reported exercising great care and forethought when formulating statements and answering questions to ensure that their language choices strengthened rather than minimized their power. The
women also described the need for extreme tact when challenging a
colleague's conclusion or interpretation of a scientific or engineering
problem.

Dale: In this male-dominated world, as much as I want to
               say, "No, you're wrong; here's technically why I'm
               right, or why this concept is right ..."—that usu-
               ally does not get you anywhere. I think it's painful
               for me to admit, and I would never admit this to
               a twelve-year-old girl, but sometimes you have to
               come across as slightly less of an expert than you

really are to get the other person to see what the situation is. I have a natural instinct to say this is *X*; this is *Y*. *X* equals this. *Y* equals that. I have to pause and think, *Okay, if I want this person to react in this way, here is what life has taught me to get them to react in this way.* When you are a minority in a technical field, it works the best to get the reactions that you want. It's choosing what you're going to say and how you're going to say it to accomplish your desired outcome, which is the goal, not just to appease but to keep moving forward.

Alice: When I speak with my managers for performance evaluations, I always say, "Well, I'm just very interested in having a progressive career. I want to make sure I have forward career momentum." I never say things like, "I want to be a VP," or "I see myself as the head therapeutic area leader," or "I see myself as a CEO in time." I always use the word "progressive career." I use those kinds of terms as opposed to, "When are you going to promote me?" Which, I think, can result in a(n) "Oh God, she's in here every three months looking for a promotion" type thing. I use language that conveys what I'm talking about, but I'm not being overt.

Randi: I'm on the introverted side of the scale, but I aggressively look for opportunities to speak up in meetings. You have to be part of the conversation or else you are perceived as someone who's not particularly interested.

Alice: Even in the language you use and in the jokes that you make, you must make it seem like you are part of that club. For example, I was invited to speak to a very senior group about my program, and when I arrived, there was only one seat at the table, and

I thought, "I'm sitting there." I joked to the senior leader, "Now I know where all the smart women at the company are. They're all here at your team." I think that put the leader and me on a level as colleagues rather than, "Oh, thank you so much for asking me to come and present."

Susan: It's about practicing that public performance and how one speaks, how one carries oneself, what one wears—the whole package. It's different here in the biotech industry. In the academic setting, looks don't seem to matter that much. At least that's my impression. Gray hair or an untidy haircut doesn't go down as well here as in the academic setting, where that aspect doesn't seem to matter as much.

Three of the women in the study suggested that it was important to be cautious about explanations regarding home-related issues that might be viewed through a negatively tinted gender lens. The women agreed that offering a child-care reason for not attending a meeting was viewed differently and negatively when it came from a woman but positively when it came from a man.

Susan: In this environment, being somewhat enigmatic actually can be quite helpful; not to be a complete see-through, and to carry all the emotions on one's face or give too much information. For example, if day care says your child is sick, and you have to leave, what do you say? Do you really say your child is sick, and my husband can't go because his job is more important? Or do you say, "I'm just going to work from home in the afternoon," and not give an explanation? If you're a father and say, "I'm going to my daughter's ballet performance at 3:00 p.m., I can't go to this meeting," you're the best dad in the world, but if you're a mother, you're a slacker.

Mary:	I learned a long time ago that if you can't go to a meeting because of a personal or child-related obligation, you don't tell them why. It's, "I can't make that meeting. I have a conflict." And most times you are not going to be asked what it is. I think women tend to say, "Oh, I have a school thing; my kid's sick," whatever. Being that transparent is something men don't do.
Alice:	While I was pregnant, I never once used the term "pregnancy brain." Ever. I never used lack of sleep as an excuse; never did any of that.

Impression management: associations and affiliations. Three of the participants, all from different STEM fields, stated that the groups with which one chooses to affiliate played a part in impression management. Gender-based stereotypes were important to recognize and to avoid.

Karen:	I refused to be involved in any kind of organization that was all women. I refused to do Junior League. I refused to do women's networking clubs, and there were all kinds of them out there when I was starting. And I said, this is just not what I want to do. I refused to do that.
Interviewer:	And your rationale for that was ...?
Karen:	I call them MOLs, "moms on the lawn." It really, really bugs me when a woman goes to college, works hard, gets a degree, and then never does anything with it. Probably two-thirds of my neighborhood did just that. And they would be sitting in their lawn chairs as their kids were walking home from school, sipping who knows what. We call them MOLs,

moms on the lawn. I didn't want to be associated in any way with that image.

Randi: It really doesn't do you any good to be part of the coffee klatch. The insights that you might get into some of the current events are not worth the poor perception of you for being part of that group.

Interviewer: What do you think that perception is?

Randi: I think it's stereotypical of women sort of flock together. They all go to the ladies' room together. So I don't want to be perceived as part of that group. It's important to stand on your own and make your own decisions.

Alice: I think there are things that are unconscious, like the company you keep. Because I'm a new mom, I have more in common from a social perspective with people at lower levels within the organization who are more my comfort group. So I have to consciously go out of my way to see who has just been promoted to SVP in corporate strategy and to reach out to them and make a lunch appointment. I really need to be acting like, "I'm one of you guys," with people at senior levels, and that has to be really, really conscious. But I feel like when you're given a certain power, if you don't use it, it's taken away from you.

Impression management: adapt and adjust. Many of the women observed that the imperative to adapt and adjust behavior appeared to fall within the domain of the women in STEM and not the men. While they recognized this as unfair, they did not allow these disparate expectations to stall their forward progress.

Yasmin: When you work with a bunch of men, you have to adapt. It's not fair because why don't they adapt, right? But its fine; it can be done. They may not know how to talk to me, but I can learn how to talk to them. So that's what I've done, is adapt, and then you change your behavior. And sometimes it's the way you sit at the table; sometimes it's how you participate in a meeting just to make sure you're heard, and sometimes you have to try many times until you make sure you are finally able to talk. But you have to get it done. And eventually, that pays off.

Impression management: differentiate yourself. The participants shared the belief that differentiating oneself in a positive way was an important success strategy. Differentiating activities included roles, appearance, and behaviors.

Tess: A mentor of mine said, "You can't get into academia now just by being good at what you do; you have to differentiate." So you differentiate by either going into basic science, clinical research, and you go to the best place you can—so I went to Harvard. You have to differentiate, or you will just be seen as a piece of plankton. You're very necessary to the ecosystem, right? But there's very little that differentiates you from the next piece of plankton, and there's a piece of plankton that's willing and able to take your place. I ended up being an instructor at Harvard, and that has served me well as a differentiator.

Sabine: If I'm going to be in a meeting where I am the only female, I emphasize that. I wear bright colors. It does allow you to differentiate yourself visually from the sea of homogeny behind you. I've also found that if you are the one sitting in the front in the bright color, people are more likely to expect you to speak up.

Claire: I had a really good mentor, a woman, early in my career when I was managing projects, going to client
meetings where everybody in the room was a man.
She gave me some simple advice and said, "When
you're running the meeting or if you have something to say, stand up." Standing up was very important advice because it's a physical manifestation.
You get eyes on you. You're not hanging back in the
shadows. And then you can just be competent, but
you've taken charge. That was very good advice.

Political Skill

**Theme 11: "Develop skills in networking, negotiating, communi-
cating, and interpersonal savvy."** All of the participants in this study
work in organizations and reported that political skills were a necessary
competency for successfully overcoming the gender-based barriers they
faced.

Political skill in this study falls within the category of social effectiveness and includes the constructs of social intelligence, social skill,
and social competence (Ferris, Treadway, Perrewé, Brouer, Douglas,
and Lux 2007). Five behavioral subsets of political skill emerged from
the data: (a) visibility and networking, (b) negotiating, (c) crafting communications, (d) interpersonal savvy, and (e) empathy.

Alice: Political skills are critical, really critical. Political
skills for me come under two buckets. One element
is navigating the organization and knowing who
you need to align with, and how you get something
done, and how you get the leader on your side before
the meeting. I think the second element is more the
interpersonal skills, so that you really understand

the other person's agenda. Even before you have the meeting, maybe it's more of like a negotiation skill, but that you really understand what that person wants, and what you want, and what your desired outcome is. And what the best way to get to that desired outcome is, and how you can achieve your desired outcome at the same time as making them look good.

Political skill: visibility and networking. The women in this study frequently mentioned the importance of visibility within the organization to career growth. Participants mentioned that they seized opportunities to speak, to lead initiatives, and to participate in activities in which senior leaders were involved, and that these endeavors created visibility opportunities.

Alice: I figured out that I had to make my own connections. I had to sell myself to other people. I had to reach out to them, raise my hand, and say, "I understand you've got this great project. I'd like to work for you on it." And there was nothing to keep that from happening. I realized I had to develop other relationships and work-arounds.

Karen: I'm fairly social. When the firm was trying to grow the business, they had a speaker come in, a CPA, who told us to go out there and be a rainmaker, to network. He said you should take a banker to lunch each week. And you should take an attorney to lunch each week. I decided I'm going do that. And I did. I started really pounding the pavement. The others didn't really do it very much. What the guys did was go play golf with their friends. I ended up bringing in more business than anyone else.

Sabine: One thing that's been critical to my success is be-
                   ing willing to make connections and do things for
                   other people that don't necessarily benefit you in
                   the moment. I think of it as farming. Respecting
                   the contribution that everyone can bring is import-
                   ant. I'm willing to be the person that sifts through
                   and makes the originator feel valued and give the
                   implementers the nuggets that they need to move
                   forward. Being willing to take the time to bring out
                   the best in other people is an important approach.

Gina: Exposure is highly valued, at least here, because
                   that's how people move up. If people know you, you
                   move up. If they don't know you, regardless of your
                   abilities, it doesn't matter. If you are in your office
                   working like a slave, they don't know.

Political skill: negotiating. Participants named negotiating skills
as a subset of political skills and gave examples of how critically important negotiating skills were to accomplishing desired outcomes.
Negotiating skills were utilized both internally within the organization
and externally with clients and partners.

Clair: Recently I wanted to hire a biologist, so I opened up
                   a biologist position. Another manager of biologists
                   immediately sent flame mail to all kinds of people
                   saying, "She shouldn't be doing that. We should be
                   hiring this person in our group. She shouldn't be
                   doing it in her group." And he just made a big stink.

                   So instead of confronting him, I acknowledged his
                   concern, acknowledged that, yes, he did have biolo-
                   gists who did these particular things and that he had
                   every right to be unhappy about what I was doing
                   and that I would change the position description
                   so that it doesn't match what his biologists do. And

what could he do? Once we hire the biologist, this biologist is going do whatever we want, and I win. So I got what I wanted, by not confronting him, by acknowledging his ego, his empire, his territory. And by making some nonmaterial concessions, I still got what I wanted. I hadn't thought about what I did with the biologist hire as a mitigating behavior. But it certainly was.

Alice: We have a collaboration with another company for our medical products. It is a young company, and their medical director wants to look good amongst his peers. I know that what will make me look good at my company is getting things done. I think you need to give a little and decide, "What do I really want out of this situation? What could the person that's a barrier to me achieve that he needs, and how can I give that to him and at the same time achieve my objective?" So I will be complimentary about the medical director and say in the large meeting, "Steve made this wonderful comment that we've incorporated here. I really think it makes this document a lot stronger; thank you so much, Steve. Are there any other comments? No? Done."

Political skill: crafting communications. The women in this study defined political behavior broadly and included the ability to read others and shift their behavior accordingly. All of the women in the study were familiar with their Myers Briggs Type Indicator® preferences. They discussed knowing and using the knowledge of the communication and influencing approaches that were most effective with people whose MBTI preferences were different from their own.

Ann: I found that framing things in a different context, taking the question and putting it in different terms they could relate to and talking to them ("them" being whoever it was who was controlling my ability to do what I needed to do) in a language that they would understand was important. I remember going to one of the deans knowing that he wasn't going to feel comfortable that I was asking for the opportunity to lead this new initiative. And I said to him, "I know that I'm not the person that you want to have do it, but let me. I know you're the quarterback. I know that you wanted to throw the ball to so and so, but he's covered; he can't catch it. I know your second choice would have been so and so, but he fell down." I said, "Give me the ball and I will run with it." You couldn't react to those feelings that made you feel like you were being discredited, demeaned sometimes. You just had to keep on looking for another way to communicate with them.

Susan: Often, the concepts that you have to discuss are complex, and people come with very different backgrounds. You must try to keep it at a level where that complexity is somehow captured, but it's distilled down to the essence so that everybody can follow; and to not presume that because people are in positions of authority, they know it all.

Susan: It's the whole way of operating. There's a certain smoothness to it. Managing to talk to the right people at the right time, engaging in the social after-work behavior and not ruffling the wrong feathers. And then it helps if you're also successful with your projects, but sometimes that's outside of your control. One of the skills that I would certainly encourage my daughter to pick up any on is communication and debating skills. I think the spoken word and being very confident is something that they learn here in America much better than they do in Europe.

Sabine: I've spent quite a bit of time over the last ten years reading and trying to understand the particular skills that I bring to any given situation. In a training on social skills, I learned how versatile my communication patterns are. I confront by questioning, and that actually tends to work better for me. My favorite comment to my kids is, "Is this going to get you what you want?" I use that at work. Is this going to get you to the goal that we are all to get to as a project team, as a company, or as a whatever? And if it's not, leave it behind, and let's move forward.

The women in this study indicated that in STEM organizations, knowledge truly is power and, as such, could be used to advance one's career and one's goals and objectives.

Claire: I find that male technical experts in the math and sciences tend to think that they will be more valuable if they hoard information, if they keep knowledge to themselves. I think they have a perception that if they don't share knowledge, they'll have some unique power or some unique capability. I've learned that the opposite actually helps your advancement, that if you share everything, tell everybody everything, teach people to do what you do, teach cohorts to do what you do, that what happens is they're grateful. And then they help you out. At the times in my career when I have gotten stuck, there's always somebody that I've already helped and that has saved me multiple times.

Political skill: interpersonal savvy. The women in this study reported that the knowledge and use of interpersonal skills (i.e., insight into human needs, collaboration, use of positive and appreciative feedback, nonadversarial approaches, and humor) were extremely important to their ability to accomplish goals and achieve senior leadership roles.

Amy: My approach in life and my metaphor has always been, I always want one foot in the boat. I'm not the kind of person who's going to throw rocks at the boat from the shore; I would rather get one foot in the boat, understand how they're thinking, and figure out how to change their minds. I do it without antagonizing because antagonizing and provoking and irritating never works.

Gina: I would say that every time I've had a downfall, for whatever reason, from a political perspective in terms of gender, it's because men are easily threatened. So you have to be very careful to not threaten men—especially your boss.

Jennifer: The other attribute that some women have that does not go over well in a man's world is the aggressive behavior, which, if you were a man, it would go over well. There are women in this organization whose technical skills I respect enormously, but their communication skills are abrasive, and so they get to be known as the bitch. That's a horrible place to be. Once you're tagged that, it's really hard to shake.

                Condescending tones don't go over well either, I think. To say, "Didn't you read the report? If you read page 17 of my report, you would know that blah-blah-blah-blah." When you say that to somebody in front of your peers, it does not work. I mean, it shouldn't work if a man said it either, but I think men get the free pass and women don't.

Alice: To manage difficult situations, it helps to make your point in the lighthearted way—smart people know what you're saying; they get the message. You don't have to hit them over the head with a sledgehammer. I use it a lot. I say something that's half-in-joke, whole-in-earnest. I'll say something like, "God, you are really giving me a hard time on this. Is this my New Year gift?" It's still lighthearted, but they get it.

Amy: One of my mother's famous sayings was, "You get more with sugar than you do with vinegar." My father was confrontational. He got in arguments with people. I may get my cerebral intellect from my father, but all three of his children have been successful because of the influence of my mother's personality—because my father was not successful in his career. So that's always been my style. I want to get people on my side, and then see if we can get them to bend or can we look at it a little bit differently. I don't want to confront and yell.

Political skill: empathy. Participants indicated that an awareness of the needs, feelings, and perspectives of others was an important aspect of political skill. Studies of emotional intelligence in leadership, authentic leadership, and charismatic leadership all cite the role of empathy as a critical success factor (Kellett 2002).

Tess: I think that empathy has helped me with the political piece. I can always try to put myself in the other person's shoes, and at least understand their perspective, and that helps me, I think, respond better. I admit there are people that I've run into here that have driven me crazy, to the point where I almost just couldn't work with them, but I try very hard to hide that feeling.

Alice: A very senior leader in the company once told me, "The key for influencing without authority is empathy. Empathy is the key. Empathy is understanding what the other person is feeling, doing, and needs. If you are an empathetic person, if you understand that concept, people will follow you to the moon and back. I thought that was a really good piece of advice.

Sabine: When I was out in the field, the other thing that I did was acknowledge that we all had difficult working conditions and do what I could to mitigate those circumstances. I would always be the one who had the cooler of water or the cups of coffee when it was cold outside. I knew that could be perceived as mothering or being the girl that goes to get coffee, but I always made clear to communicate that it was my job to facilitate them being able to do their jobs. And so I never took on the persona of the mother—I clearly communicated that the things that I was doing were in pursuit of the project goals. And then there is knowing who the other people in the room are and how they might react, and even interacting with them before the meeting so you can prep them, or having them prep you, because the interactions in the room might, then, be quite different

Two participants discussed the additional pressure of maneuvering the political landscape while performing cognitively complex scientific work.

Tess: It is so complicated. The expectations, you know, sometimes I just don't get it. They want me to be Mother Theresa and Marie Curie all packaged in one. I just, I don't know that men feel the same pressure in the same way that you have to have all of this and balance everything.

Yasmin: Because it's a balance, and when you have to be, you have to be liked, but at the same time, you have to be respected. There are people that are liked, but they're not respected, and so it's a fine balance; you have to balance those things. Someone that they can say, you know what, I can work with her. But at the same time, not I can work with her because she's a nice person; no, she's a strong person that's going to get it done.

It's also, sometimes you have to be strong, so you have to know your limit so that you're not putting people down, offending them, and crossing the boundaries.

Performance

Theme 12: "You can't be equal to; you must be better than. You must overprepare, overachieve, overdeliver." The findings in this study confirm those of similar studies in which women identified consistently overperforming and exceeding performance expectations as important career advancement strategies (Borg 2010; Jepson 2010). All sixteen of the women in this study identified exceptional performance, long hours, in-depth preparation, backing up their positions by citing scientific sources, and keen process analysis as important ways they achieved senior leadership. One participant summarized the views of others when she said, "you can't be equal to; you must be better than." The participants identified five behavioral subsets of performance: (a) overpreparation, (b) availability, (c) exceeding expectations, (d) scientific knowledge, intellect, cognitive and analytical skills, and (e) being seen as the intervening variable.

Performance: overpreparation. Women in this study felt there was a definite gender disparity in the preconceived beliefs held about a woman's ability to perform in STEM, and they used intensive in-depth preparation, some called it over preparation, to demonstrate their competency.

Kate: When I go to a meeting, I do my homework, and I get a little crazy with the staff about getting things organized—where's this, where's that, we need to pull this together, where are the props? Where are the tables, where are the figures, where are the plans? Let's get this color coordination down. I need to be ready; I will not walk into a situation unprepared. A lot of times I never use the stuff, but I'll be damned if I'm going to be put on the stage and not be prepared. A guy doesn't care, and it's tolerated. If I get up there on the stage and I'm not prepared, I'm a dumb broad. I think you have to work harder, no doubt. I think you have to be technically better. I think you have to do it in the absence of benefiting from the old boys' network, since there is no girls network, not really. Just have the facts. Do your research; just make sure you're on top of the game. Because that's the difference between a man and a woman; you have to prove yourself more. It's constant, it never ends. And sometimes it's exhausting.

Ann: During rounds in medical school, being very well prepared was critically important to being taken seriously. I noticed that a male attending physician could offer his opinion about a case without any literature-based evidence, and it would be accepted. My opinions were always questioned. After a few really irritating situations, I began to prepare, extra prepare. My strategy was overpreparation and having all my ducks in a row before I would ever make an assertion. I wouldn't say anything until I absolutely knew I was right—and could prove it. Today we call it evidence-based medicine.

Vivian: Preparation was key. Preparation of the slides, introducing the topic, and level setting everybody was key. I was perceived as making people feel stupid because I didn't give enough background to people. I was assuming that everybody understood the science. If I understand, a poor immigrant, why can't they understand it? Now, I understand that not everybody comes from the same background. So, putting a lot of effort and extra work and extra slides and extra writing, really to present the case before we can discuss it in an intelligent way. That's a lot of preparation.

Performance: availability. Women in the study encountered the supposition that women with children would not be as available and/or as dedicated as men. The women had to make it clear that they could travel at a moment's notice or be available on the weekend although the participants viewed these demands as gender-based tests.

Susan: You had to show that your dedication and that you were reachable on weekends, at night, on my vacation, and that you were willing to drop as much as you could to be there.

Mary: I remember being asked by my boss, "Can you go to Dublin (Ireland) next week?" I had a ten-month-old baby at home. I called my mom, and I said, "Could you come up next week so I can go to Dublin?"

           She said, "What?" I said, "Yeah, there's this project opportunity," and she said, "Okay." So I picked up the phone and said, "Sure, I can go to Dublin next week." This was definitely a test. I could tell from the politics of the situation that this was one of those tests and, I'll defuse the politics if I can do this.

Performance: exceeding expectations. Participants provided specific examples of how exceeding performance expectations was an essential tool for overcoming gender-based perceptions and barriers.

Karen:

They figured out pretty quickly that I was a good worker and that I could get a job done, and do it well. I probably worked harder than any staff person there. I overworked. And to this day, I still do. I was not going to let anybody outshine me. So I made sure I was the first one there, the last one to leave, always had the most overtime. I was always the highest in billable hours. One day, the managing partner called in all the managers and said instead of raises this year, we will give you 10 percent of whatever business you bring in. He stopped it after six months because I was making too much money. I outperformed all the other managers. In this business, you can't dispute the numbers. But all the numbers were there.

Susan:

We've had very senior women leaders come here to talk about women's issues and how you make a career in the world of biotech and business. They shared that they gave up any sort of family life to achieve what they have achieved because they faced so many obstacles. They always had to be at the top of their game so that there's no question about performance. They always had to go the extra mile, take on extra projects, and take extra courses. So it wasn't just enough to be good at your day-to-day job; good wasn't good enough.

Women also mentioned that while excellent performance was a positive differentiator, it had to be done with finesse so as not to be perceived as "blowing your own trumpet" or inappropriate competitiveness.

Susan: You would have to excel but do it in a way that appeared humble, and appeared in a way that you weren't blowing your own trumpet. You couldn't leave any question that you had missed a single thing because if you had missed something, even if it was minor, it would come back as a huge thing for you; whereas for your male colleague who might have missed the same thing, it wouldn't have been much of an issue.

Ann: We interns typically never made it into the operating room because we were assigned so much of what was called *scut work*, a lot of work on the wards. If we finished our work on the wards, we were allowed to go to the operating room and see the surgery for which we wanted to train. I knew that if I was going to benefit in any way from all these surgical experiences, I needed to get to the operating room and see the cancers inside the patient, and try to learn something about cancer and how it was treated surgically. I got there early to get my scut work done, and I did. I was one of the few interns who made it to surgery every day. I realized that the playing field wasn't going to be level. And so I just knew that I couldn't be equal to; I would have to be better than in order to have a chance to do some of these things that I wanted to do.

Mary: I was the kind of student that needed to get an A on everything. The kind of person when I'm delivering a report to a client, that I want it to be perfect, and if it means I have to stay up all night to make it perfect, I will. I think it demonstrates two things. One is commitment to delivering really good quality results. And the other is intelligence.

Gina: I am on the high end of the performance scale. So, whether somebody finds me appealing or not, they want me when they need a job done. I may have the world's track record for ushering drugs through the regulatory process.

Jennifer: I remember when I first started working, they had trouble keeping me busy. I performed my tasks well and faster than they expected me to. They may not have had anything else to compare it to other than the men in the office who didn't produce as much. You know, it's a societal thing, because, if you're not a professional white male, you've got to do 150 percent when everybody else just gets by with 85.

Tess: One thing that I will always win the battle on is, I always know how to get things done. I will do so in an efficient way, and that will be my hook; that's my strategy. I am very organized and very disciplined. I tend to come in fairly early. So that was my strategy to be noticed. It was having that maturity of knowing how to get things done that gave me satisfaction. So I made chief resident at the hospital. I was known for getting things done and getting the teaching done. Those were some of my earliest strategies.

Achieving and maintaining a senior leadership position is not without cost.

Kate: Being a successful woman in this business has a cost. If you want to get to vice president by the time you're thirty-five, then know that you're probably not going to have a couple of kids at home and going to soccer unless you have a husband who is going to do all that for you. If you get to that level, and you don't want to keep on going up, that's okay, because that gives you the time to take care of your parents, or whatever it is, or have that family or whatever, but don't think you can have it all at the same time; you can't.

Performance: scientific knowledge, intellect, cognitive and analytical skills. Several of the women in the study cited the importance of scientific, technical, and process knowledge as a differentiating quality. Participants gave numerous examples of how the ability to assess and analyze a situation and then provide accurate diagnoses and/or workable solutions resulted in creating a perception of being an asset to the organization.

Mary: I actually think that in the science and engineering fields, there is a lot of respect for intelligence. I think more so than in some other fields. Because it's about problem solving, and if you have problem-solving skills, people recognize that. If there is a really hard problem, a math problem, a science problem, an engineering problem, and you can figure that out, that's a very good thing.

Vivian: I always believed a deep scientific knowledge could take me anywhere, regardless. I also was driven by "know your stuff well and be passionate about what you do," and everything else comes with it.

Ann: I had been through three hundred cases of lymphomas, so I knew lymphomas. I was observing a surgery, and they grabbed my arm, stuck it into the abdomen of the patient. The surgeon said, "We don't know what this is." I said, "It's a mesenteric lymphoma. Nothing else would do that to the mesentery." They looked at me like I had three eyes in my head. Immediately after I said that, the pathologist came into the room and said, "It's a diffuse large-cell mesenteric lymphoma." They all looked at me like I was a witch or something.

Sabine: I was in grad school when I learned that I was very good at framing questions and problems in ways that other people didn't see them. That has been a strength for me moving forward technically. I tend to be able to focus and distill problems and systems in a way that helps other people focus the question and get the answer. I have the ability to sit and talk through their research with them, or look at things with them and ask questions that ended up helping them get where they wanted to go. It was very empowering for me to have that skill and to help others think through what they were doing, even if it wasn't my area of technical expertise.

Gina: It's not so easy for women—I mean, maybe I'm oversimplifying it for men, but men don't have to demonstrate their competency first. I think women have to start by not only demonstrating their competency but their extreme competency.

Dale: I definitely think my intellect has been very helpful. I think that having that intellect and knowing that I have that intellect is a phenomenal combination. I wasn't given this IQ not to do anything with it. I wasn't given this problem not to find at least ten solutions, maybe thirty, maybe fifty. I always think, if I just calm down, use the brain that I was given, then I can solve this.

Karen: A lot of people don't understand numbers—they just
                don't get it. If you can hold a meeting and talk your
                numbers properly and point out the good and the
                bad and take them down the path of what needs to
                be done, they gain a lot of respect for you. I always
                start out as treasurer on all the boards that I'm on. I
                don't sit there like a dumb blonde. I speak up. I am
                always kind of out there.

Performance: be the intervening variable. Participants stated that
it was important to be recognized as someone who identifies and takes
on projects that are in trouble and then turns them around, to be the
individual who steps in to solve problems that have caused a project or a
team to become delayed, and/or to be someone who uses her particular
talents in a way that becomes the intervening variable to the success of
a project. Participants agreed that being in a lead contributor role rather
than in a support role was important.

Alice: I think it's important to take on roles where it's
                recognized that there's a disaster going on. Then,
                when you come in, you're the variable that's new.
                So if things take off, it's very difficult to credit some-
                thing outside of that. I've always actively gone out
                and looked for those opportunities—the difficult
                projects no one wants. Even my recent move—the
                group was struggling, the program was a mess, and
                it was recognized in the company. We've turned it
                around, and I think that's really what's resulted in
                my career taking off.

Dale: I like solving problems, and I like finding multi-
                ple solutions. And I think my desire to find those
                multiple solutions helps me navigate the corporate
                environment compared to those who only see one
                linear path forward.

Kate: You have to be technically better—whether it's cli-
               ent service or project management, people manage-
               ment, or whatever, you have to be better; no doubt
               about it.

Vivian: They appreciated the fact that I had covered the full
               spectrum, not focusing just on the science, but un-
               derstanding the other functions, like the commer-
               cial aspect, the taxes—things we have to consider
               when we develop products. They appreciate the fact
               that I had vetted all these issues, and I was able to
               put this study into a more complete context.

Randi: If I was designing a(n) MBA for women, I would
               make sure that they understood, "You must excel.
               You absolutely must perform. It's just expected."

Ann: When we first started treating patients at the new fa-
               cility, I knew there was a problem, a big process gap.
               I was told, "We're never going to make the projec-
               tions that you predicted." I asked, "Why not? Why
               can't we?" There were a thousand reasons about
               why we could not achieve the kind of throughput
               that our projections had required. So I stood down
               in the treatment rooms, and with my watch, and
               paid attention to all the places where time was be-
               ing lost. I went back and said, "You need another
               therapist on the machine. We have to reorganize
               the operation around optimizing beam time." I
               showed that we had to think about this differently.
               Our goal was to have an average room turnover
               time of twenty minutes—we made it to thirteen
               minutes. We are now more than able to make our
               financial operational goals, and since we've been so
               far ahead of the curve, we've been allowed to func-
               tion the way we want to function.

Summary

This study was designed to explore the phenomenon addressed in the central research question: What are the lived experiences of women in STEM senior leadership using buffering behaviors to overcome gender bias and achieve success? All sixteen participants reported encountering discriminatory and hostile gender-based treatment in STEM. These successful women, all of whom hold senior leadership positions in STEM, are distinguished by their highly developed sense of self-efficacy. As a result, when dealing with gender-based discrimination, they all reported the use of buffering behaviors (self-monitoring, impression management, political skill, and performance) to mitigate the gender-based hostility. Chapter 5 presents an in-depth analysis and structural synthesis of the themes, subcategories, and behavioral subsets revealed by the data.

Summary, Conclusions, and Recommendations

Statement of the Problem

Despite fifty years of equal opportunity legislation and initiatives, women are still significantly underrepresented in leadership roles throughout corporate organizations, government, and society, particularly in the fields of science, technology, engineering, and mathematics (STEM). Women have demonstrated that they have the skill, talent, and experience to contribute to organizational success; however, their path to leadership is frequently blocked (Hewlett et al. 2008; Wentling & Thomas 2007). This problem affects both organizations and people because it limits access to a broad array of insights, experiences, and knowledge at the senior level where leaders are making strategic decisions and formulating corporate direction. Minimizing the contributions of any group of talented individuals can lead to cognitive oversights in discovery, problem solving, and innovation. Global competition, especially in science and technology, is rapidly growing, and corporate entities are under increasing pressure to produce innovative solutions and financial results (Hewlett et al. 2008).

Purpose, Theoretical Framework, and Conceptual Elements of the Study

This purpose of this chapter is to synthesize and discuss the results of this phenomenological study in light of the research goals, the theoretical framework, the methodology, the literature review, and the conceptual elements. While chapter 4 presented the themes, subcategories, and behavioral subsets that emerged from the shared lived experiences of the participants, chapter 5 presents an analysis and synthesis of the meaning of these themes. Chapter 5 will also describe the strengths and weaknesses of the study, offer recommendations for future research, and discuss the relevance of the findings to women striving to reach leadership positions in STEM organizations.

The purpose of this study was to explore the research question, what are the lived experiences of women in STEM senior leadership using buffering behaviors to overcome gender bias and achieve success? The study explored the essence and meaning of the lived experiences of senior women leaders who have utilized buffering behaviors to overcome gender-based barriers and have achieved positions of leadership in the traditionally male-dominated fields of science, technology, engineering, or mathematics (STEM). The data revealed recurring themes and patterns that illuminated the phenomenon of encountering gender discrimination, bias and exclusion, the vital role that self-efficacy played in women's success, and the development and use of buffering behaviors by women as they overcame gender-based bias and achieved leadership roles in STEM. What makes this phenomenological study unique is that it focuses exclusively on the views and experiences of women who have encountered gender-based discrimination and marginalization and who persevered to attain positions of leadership in STEM organizations.

This study incorporated a feminist epistemology that informs a critical theory paradigm. The goal of a critical advocacy paradigm is the empowerment of individuals and the discovery of knowledge that could lead to change (Ponterotto 2005). A feminist theory perspective ensures that women's viewpoints, experiences, and perspectives are equally valued and reflected (Brooks & Hesse-Biber 2007; Landman 2006).

The theoretical framework of the study was based on Bandura's social cognitive theory (Bandura 1994, 2001; Bandura, Caprara, Barbaranelli, Bussey & Bandura 1999; Chen 2006; Gerbino & Pastorelli 2003), which holds that individuals can consciously learn and choose behaviors that will influence outcomes within their environments. This foundational theory served as a lens through which the researcher examined and analyzed the data collected, both from the literature and from the participants. Two aspects of social cognitive theory, self-regulation and self-efficacy, emerged as essential components of success for the women in the study.

The conceptual elements of this study are presented in three main areas: (a) the role of self-efficacy in the use of buffering behaviors, (b) the gender-based barriers encountered in STEM that create the need for buffering behaviors, and (c) examples of the buffering behaviors women employed to overcome gender-based barriers. The sources of self-efficacy and the use of self-efficacious behaviors provided important insights into the beliefs and actions that sustained the women in the study as they confronted gender bias, resistance, and marginalization. The conceptual elements of masculine hegemony, gender bias, gender backlash, and gendered organizations frame the experiences of the gender-based hostility, barriers, and obstacles encountered by the women in the study. Examples of the challenges women encountered are juxtaposed against the buffering behaviors that women developed and utilized to overcome these challenges in order to pursue their careers in STEM, and their desire to lead and make meaningful contributions. The buffering behaviors include self-monitoring, impression management, political skill, and performance.

The participants included sixteen highly educated women from the fields of science, technology, engineering, and mathematics. Of the sixteen, five participants hold medical degrees, one participant holds both an MD degree and a PhD degree, one participant holds a degree in mathematics and a PhD in systems engineering, six have master's degrees (one in structural engineering, one in geotechnical engineering, one in systems design and management, one in chemistry, and one in geology), three hold bachelor's degrees in civil and/or environmental engineering and are certified professional engineers, one is a CPA who owns her own business. Participants all had a minimum of three years in their leadership roles and have decision-making authority over others.

The criterion for an effective phenomenological research interview is "as complete a description as possible of the experience the participant has lived through" (Giorgi 2009, 122). Interviews elicited participants' stories, perceptions, feelings, opinions, and beliefs about their experiences with using buffering behaviors to overcome gender discrimination and provided the focal point of data collection in this study. The researcher used Seidman's (2013) three-stage interview model for phenomenological inquiry. The first stage is a "focused life history" (Seidman 2013, 21) that inquires about experiences from the participant's past. The second stage focuses on the details of the participant's experiences in the present, and the third stage asks the participant to reflect on the meaning of her experiences with the phenomenon (Seidman 2013).

Discussion of Findings and Structural Synthesis of Themes

Three major categories of phenomena emerged from this study and included (a) the unifying theory of role of self-efficacy in the use of buffering behaviors by women leaders in STEM, (b) the gender-based barriers women encountered that required the use of buffering behaviors in STEM organizations and cultures, and (c) specific description of the buffering behaviors that women leaders in STEM employed to advance in their careers. This study examined four gender-based barriers that women most often encountered in male-dominated professions—the masculine stereotype of leadership and hegemony, gender bias, gender backlash, and gendered organizations. The four buffering behaviors examined in the study included self-awareness, impression management, performance, and political skill.

Twelve themes were identified. The phenomena of self-efficacy produced four themes: theme 1: early messages and experiences, theme 2: athletic experiences and/or physical challenges, theme 3: positive self-talk, and theme 4: taking control of one's career destiny. Four themes emerged from the phenomena of gender-based barriers: theme 5: STEM is a man's world—power will not be shared nor given to women, theme 6: a prevailing belief that women can't and won't perform well in STEM, theme 7: you won't last—we'll freeze you out, and theme 8: you don't belong here—you are not welcome here. Specific examples of the buffering behaviors that participants employed to overcome gender-based barriers generated four themes: theme 9: be self-aware and alert; theme 10: perceive, analyze, modify, evaluate, adjust; theme 11: networks, negotiating, communicating, and interpersonal savvy; and theme 12: intellect is not enough—overprepare, overachieve, and overdeliver. What follows is a discussion of the meaning of each of the themes in light of the original research question and within the context of the current literature and the theoretical framework.

Unifying Theory of Self-Efficacy: Four Themes

The data showed that the unifying theory of self-efficacy was central to women's perseverance toward their leadership goals in the face of gender-based exclusion, verbal abuse, and mistreatment. An individual's judgment of self-efficacy determines the amount and the duration of effort he or she will expend in the face of obstacles and adverse experiences (Bandura 1982). Self-efficacy mechanisms influence the choice and execution of courses of actions required to deal with situations (Bandura 1982). Self-efficacy encompasses "people's beliefs about their capabilities to produce designated levels of performance that exercise influence over events that affect their lives (Bandura 1994, 71). An individual's level of self-efficacy determines his or her likelihood to enter into challenging situations, to persist in the face of setbacks, and to find ways to achieve desired outcomes (Bandura 2001). The lived experiences of the participants consistently supported the findings reported in the literature on self-efficacy.

Self-Efficacy Theme 1: Early Messages and Experiences

Self-efficacy, the deep belief in one's ability to act upon and influence the outcome of a situation, developed early in the lives of the participants. Affirming messages from significant people in the early lives of participants and early experiences of responsibility appear to have been a primary source of this essential foundational element of self-efficacy in the women's belief systems. Their beliefs of self-efficacy enabled them to persevere toward their career goals in science, technology, engineering, and mathematics in the face of gender-based obstacles. Research has shown that parents influence a child's career choice primarily by the impact they have on the child's development of self-efficacy (Bandura, Barbaranelli, Caprara, & Pastorelli 2001). A study of 272 children examined sociocognitive influences that shape children's career aspirations and found that a child's perceived self-efficacy is more likely to determine career choice and path than actual academic achievement (Bandura, Barbaranelli, Caprara, & Pastorelli 2001).

The importance of self-efficacy in the success of the participants cannot be overstated. The beliefs that "you can do anything" and "you are as smart as or smarter than the men that are holding you back" provided the necessary fuel that enabled these women to persevere in the face of the demeaning and blatantly sexist treatment they frequently encountered. Participants credited parents and teachers for instilling these early beliefs in their abilities and rights and provided a strong foundation that sustained them in difficult times. Participants who were parents expressed a determination to do the same for their children.

    Structural synthesis of theme 1: early messages and experiences. Most of the participants are parents, and, during the interviews, they expressed a newfound realization of how important parental messages were to their own development of self-efficacy and vowed to do the same for their children. One participant recalled being driven to an interview for an internship with NASA by her father. As she exited the car he said, "Just remember, you can do anything." She said that whenever she is in doubt, she recalls that day and gains strength and confidence from the memory. Another participant remembers walking with her grandmother, a nurse, and telling her that she wanted to be a nurse someday too. Her grandmother replied, "You can be a doctor if you want. You can do whatever you want to do. It's up to you to decide what you want to do and make it happen." This conversation took place when the participant was five years old, and she recalls it vividly as a shaping moment in her life. As Wordsworth wrote (1888): "The child is father of the man"—and woman.

Self-Efficacy Theme 2: Athletic Experiences and/or Physical Challenges

Athletic experiences and/or physical challenges provided opportunities for the participants in this study to develop self-efficacy. The women in this study reported that participating in athletic activities provided the opportunity to set and reach goals, to meet and overcome challenges, to have control over one's actions and behaviors, and to work with and lead teams. Developing these skills early in life provided important foundational insights and experiences that enabled participants to confront the competitive challenges they faced in male-dominated STEM organizations. This theme was unexpected but mentioned frequently enough to warrant inclusion as a theme. As Claire stated, "I think it's important for girls and young women to have some kind of challenge that they step up and take on. And then you know that in your bones that you can do that."

The data revealed in theme 2 supports the findings in the literature. One of the most influential sources of self-efficacy is derived from experiences of mastery (Bandura 1997). Studies have shown that participation in men's and women's intercollegiate sports contributes to leadership development (Handel 1993). Sports and physical challenges offer the opportunity to work toward and achieve goals, which can become a mastery experience for a young girl and promote feelings of self-efficacy (Cole 2014). Girls who develop athletic skills in early adolescence were found to have heightened self-esteem (Hage-Cameron 2003). Several women cited the competitive athletic opportunities created by the passage of Title IX legislation in 1972 as an important milestone for them in college and expressed regret that the implementation of Title IX continues to be debated and disputed.

Structural synthesis of theme 2: athletic and/or physical challenges. An unexpected finding of this study was the preponderance of evidence regarding the positive influence on women's beliefs of self-efficacy that came from athletic competition or physical challenges. These recollections were in answer to the open-ended question "what other factors in your life provided you a sense of self-confidence?" Over half of the participants recalled feelings of accomplishment, achievement, and power when playing team sports such as tennis, soccer, rugby, and softball, and individual sports such as long distance running, swimming, and track and field events. One woman told of her daughter's growth in self-esteem after captaining and navigating a boat to safety in the midst of a bad storm during an Outward Bound experience. The woman said the difference in her daughter was transformational.

Self-Efficacy Theme 3: Positive Self-Talk

Women's beliefs of self-efficacy were operationalized through the use of positive self-talk, a conscious internal conversation in which women reminded themselves of their highly developed capabilities and encouraged themselves to persevere. The literature provides extensive evidence of the effect of positive self-talk on performance (Gould & Weiss 1981; Hamilton, Scott, & MacDougall 2007; Hatzigeorgiadis 2006). Self–talk is a conscious and cognitive activity that incorporates both motivating and instructional statements although motivational statements have shown to have greater positive impact on enhancing performance and limiting critical thoughts (Hatzigeorgiadis 2006). When confronted with gender-based inequities, the women in this study reported that they relied on internal dialogues to remind themselves that they had the right, the knowledge, the experience, and the competency to be leaders and to pursue their goal of leadership in STEM organizations.

Structural synthesis of theme 3: positive self-talk—"I know I can do this—this is where I belong." The importance of internal dialogue and positive self-talk was another cognitive skill that the women leaders in this study reported using extensively. All participants reported using positive self-talk, which appeared to serve as an internal source of encouragement when external sources of encouragement were absent, as was often the case. Alice, a medical doctor, provided a vivid example of self-talk: "I have this mantra that I say to myself if I'm thinking, *Oh, maybe I can't do it.* I think, *Remember you were top of your class at Harvard. You didn't dream that. You didn't imagine that. You can do this.*"

The importance of using internal dialogues that recounted factual episodes and historical evidence of past success emerged as an important success strategy employed by the participants as they faced difficult circumstances that created self-doubt. As scientists, they used evidence and data to refute flawed hypotheses about their performance capabilities.

Self-Efficacy Theme 4: Take Control of Your Career and Destiny

An individual's judgment of self-efficacy also determines the amount and the duration of effort he or she will expend in the face of obstacles and adverse experiences (Bandura 1982). Self-efficacy mechanisms influence the choice and execution of courses of actions required to deal with situations (Bandura 1982). Self-efficacy was instrumental in the participants' persistence in the face of obstacles, their proactive problem solving when they discovered unequal treatment such as pay discrepancies, their confidence to undertake difficult assignments, and their courage to take control of their own career paths and to leave untenable situations. The women in this study reported that their beliefs of self-efficacy empowered them to act in self-efficacious ways. When confronted with unfair and discriminatory actions, the women initiated and enacted remedies to indefensible situations.

Structural synthesis of theme 4: take control of your career and destiny. Self-efficacious behavior was instrumental in the ability of participants to successfully confront challenging situations, be persistent, and achieve long-held goals. The common theme was the need to take control of one's own destiny. The participants agreed that they rarely found senior male leaders who would openly champion and/or advocate for them, so they determined that career growth would have to be self-directed. As Yasmin observed, "You can't hang back and wait to be noticed. It's not enough to do a good job. If you don't take control of your life, you don't get opportunities, and it's not because people don't want to give them to you, it's because they don't know you want them. You have to ask."

Gender-Based Barriers in STEM: Four Themes

The conceptual themes of the masculine stereotype of leadership and male hegemony, gender bias, gender schema, and gendered organizations appeared to be interrelated and interwoven throughout the experiences of women in STEM. Participants in this study reported experiences from each of these categories of gender-based obstacles and challenges. The masculine stereotype of leadership and male hegemony, gender bias, gender schema, and gendered organizations all produced inhospitable environments that lead to the unequal treatment of women in male-dominated professions (Brooks & Hesse-Biber 2007; Eagly & Karau 2002; Glick & Fiske 2001; Heilman 2001; Weele & Heilman 2005). The data revealed that these participants confronted gender-based barriers that included verbal abuse, sexual harassment, intimidation, pay and promotion differentials, exclusion, and insubordination. In the face of these challenges, participants developed responses, strategies, and behaviors that enabled them to overcome these barriers and eventually reach leadership positions in STEM organizations.

Every woman in the study reported experiencing gender-based discriminatory behaviors, beliefs, decisions, and actions and that it caught them by surprise. These experiences ranged from caustic, degrading, and demeaning remarks to sexually aggressive behavior and an actual attempted assault by an attending physician upon one of the women when she was a medical student. Participants gave examples of pay differentials for the same work, the role of the good old boy club in promotions, and exclusion from career-enhancing networks. All of the participants reported being taken aback by these discriminatory actions and behaviors since they happened in respected professional organizations (universities, hospitals, research facilities, and engineering firms) and were being perpetrated by highly educated peers with advanced academic degrees in science, technology, engineering, and mathematics. An interesting common decision was that none of the women ever filed charges of sexual harassment or unfair labor practices, nor did they seek third-party interventions from Human Resources or external regulatory agencies. They stated that they had consciously chosen to compete on a male-dominated playing field and that they would find or develop ways to succeed without asking for outside interventions.

Gender-Based Barrier Theme 5: "STEM Is a Man's World—Power Will Not Be Shared nor Given to Women."

The pervasiveness of the opposition to women in STEM, the extensiveness of the antagonism toward them, and the prevalence of rancor on the part of certain men in power was unexpected by the women in the study, and they reported being shocked into silence when they first encountered these experiences. Male hegemony provides a construct within which to examine the experiences of women as they seek to achieve positions of senior leadership in science, technology, engineering, and mathematics (STEM) (Page, Bailey, & VanDelinder 2009).

Of particular interest in this area of masculinity research is that those who belong to the hegemonic group (in this case males), generally do not question the culture and policies that maintain hegemony (Page, Bailey, & VanDelinder 2009; Sheridan & Milgate 2003). The theory of masculine hegemony also provides a framework for understanding sexual harassment as a way to "police and penalize" women who challenge their subordinate position in male-dominated professions. Evidence suggests that harassment is most frequently found in male-dominated work environments and professions (McLaughlin, Uggen, & Blackstone 2012). The data support these findings.

The literature offers evidence of numerous gender-based barriers that have their origin in masculine hegemony, "the maintenance of practices that allowed men's dominance over women to continue" (Connell & Messerschmidt 2005, 832). Male hegemony provides a construct within which to examine the experiences of women as they seek to achieve positions of senior leadership in science, technology, engineering, and mathematics (Page, Bailey, & VanDelinder 2009).

Women reported episodes of hazing and mistreatment at the hands of male supervisors who did not want them in the organization. They also found that their male peers and colleagues would watch silently and not speak up to challenge inappropriate behavior. Many women reported incidents when they felt they were alone in the battle to achieve their career aspirations.

All sixteen of the study participants reported experiencing gender-based discriminatory practices and forms of sexual harassment either during their academic preparation or in the workplace. Evidence suggests that harassment most often occurs in male-dominated work settings (McLaughlin, Uggen, & Blackstone 2012). Women in careers that are not traditionally associated with the female gender are perceived as threats by the men in the profession and are, therefore, targets of sexual harassment (Kohlman 2004). Two explanations for sexual harassment in the workplace are the dominance perspective and the sex role spillover perspective (Kohlman 2004). The dominance perspective holds that sexual harassment is a means by which men in positions of authority maintain power over women and is used to "insult, deride, and degrade women" (Kohlman 2004, 145). In the sex role spillover explanation, men continue to perceive women in the traditional gender-based roles of mothers, wives, and daughters, and have difficulty relating to them as professional colleagues, peers, or equals (Kohlman 2004). Additionally, sex-role spillover contains an element of resentment found toward women who have entered male-dominated professions because they have violated the domain of men and "wrongfully left their proper role in the domestic sphere" (Kohlman 2004, 146).

Structural Synthesis of Theme 5: "STEM Is A Man's World—Power Will Not Be Shared nor Given to Women."

When the women in this study encountered demeaning, mean-spirited, and hostile behaviors including sexual coercion, they often questioned what they had done to precipitate these behaviors. The participants recognized that they were confronting gender-based power differentials and were often at a loss as to how to respond. Many of these incidents occurred during their university preparation or early in their careers. However, the women drew strength from their self-efficacious beliefs and behaviors and continued to persevere toward their goals. One participant likened the experience to a Persian proverb: "The eagle can only rise if the wind is against it." She observed, "The wind that's against you can actually provide uplift." Many of the women in this study reported that facing and overcoming gender-based obstacles and discriminatory treatment strengthened and equipped them for the next set of challenges.

Gender-Based Barrier Theme 6: "Women Can't and Won't Perform Well in STEM."

Gender bias is the antipathy directed toward women who seek positions of power that men traditionally hold (Glick & Fiske 2001). Gender bias in organizations often leads to the unequal treatment of women as they compete in male-dominated professions (Brooks & Hesse-Biber 2007; Eagly & Karau 2002; Glick & Fiske 2001; Heilman 2001; Weele & Heilman 2005). In studies on formal and informal forms of gender bias and discrimination, one of the most common obstacles reported by women was "an inhospitable corporate culture (Weele & Heilman 2005, 31). Heilman's lack of fit model (2001) and Rudman's status incongruity hypothesis (2012) provide evidence of prevalent gendered beliefs regarding the different social and organizational roles of men and of women. Gender bias in organizations often leads to the unequal treatment of women as they compete in male-dominated professions (Brooks & Hesse-Biber 2007; Eagly & Karau 2002; Glick & Fiske 2001; Heilman 2001; Weele & Heilman 2005).

Despite being told directly by men who had authority over them that women did not belong in STEM professions, these self-efficacious women continued to work toward their goals of leadership. Representative comments made to them included, "there is no place in medicine for a woman," or "the field is no place for a woman," or "go back to the kitchen where you belong," or "you should be home with your children; you don't belong here."

Structural synthesis of theme 6: "Women can't and won't perform well in stem." The degree of the hostility directed at the women who first entered STEM was surprising in a field that prides itself on objectivity and evidence. Women were told, "there is no place in medicine for a woman," or "the field is no place for a woman," or "go back to the kitchen where you belong," or "you should be home with your children, you don't belong here." While these insults were hurtful, offensive, and wounding, the universal internal response on behalf of the women was, "Oh yeah? Watch me." The tenacity and resilience of these women permeated the data. The source of their self-determination appeared to be their highly developed beliefs of self-efficacy. The participants each reported developing an array of mitigating buffering behaviors that enabled them to succeed in the face of these gender-based discriminatory episodes.

Gender based barrier theme 7: "You won't last. We'll freeze you out. You will be ill treated for violating gender stereotypes." The third conceptual element of the study encompasses a double bind that aspiring women often face, known as gender backlash (Garcia-Retamero & Lopez-Zafra 2006; Heilman, Wallen, Fuchs, & Tamkins 2004; O'Neill & O'Reilly 2011). Rudman and Fairchild (2004) introduced the concept of gender backlash and defined it as "social and economic sanctions for counter-stereotypical behavior" (Rudman & Fairchild 2004, 157;

Rudman, Moss-Racusin, Phelan, & Nauts 2012, 166). Extensive research on gender backlash has shown that when women incorporate behaviors that are considered masculine such as self-promotion, hard negotiating, competiveness, or assertiveness, they are frequently viewed negatively and not selected for senior leadership roles (Glick 2001; Gupta 2013; Heilman, Wallen, Fuchs, & Tamkins 2004; Moss-Racusin & Rudman 2010; O'Neill & O'Reilly 2011; Rudman, Moss-Racusin, Phelan, & Nauts 2012). The status incongruity hypothesis (SIH) maintains that when women violate feminine gender stereotypes they will often experience backlash through economic and social sanctions (Eagly & Karau 2002; O'Neill & O'Reilly 2011; Rudman, Moss-Racusin, Phelan, & Nauts 2012).

All sixteen participants in the study encountered gender-based barriers and degrees of gender backlash as they sought to achieve senior leadership positions. Many of the participants found that these barriers and behaviors persisted even after they attained senior leadership roles. STEM represents a highly gendered professional field in which women repeatedly encountered exclusion, devaluation, harassment, and hostility. However, the participants developed behaviors, beliefs, and approaches that enabled them to pursue and achieve their goals.

Structural synthesis of theme 7: "You won't last. We'll freeze you out. You will be ill treated for violating gender stereotypes." While all sixteen participants in the study encountered gender-based bias, mistreatment, and abuse even after they attained senior leadership roles with significant power, they persevered. STEM represents a highly gendered professional field in which women repeatedly encountered exclusion, devaluation, harassment, and hostility. What characterizes these *positive deviants* is that they did not give up; they did not quit—they were tenacious in the face of disheartening and demoralizing situations. On occasion, they become discouraged, angry, incensed, and frustrated. However, they continued to direct their energy and their intellect toward solving for X in the Y domain.

Gender-based barrier theme 8: "You don't belong here; you are unwelcome here." Organizations that grant power to some and not to others based on class, gender, and race create "inequality regimes" (Acker 2006, 443). Gender schema theories and theories of gendered organizations indicate that women seeking positions of leadership in male-dominated professions often encounter these "inequality regimes" (Acker 2006, 443) and report that they do not feel as though they fit and that they do not belong (Acker 2006; Lemons, & Parzinger 2007; Ridgeway 2009). Descriptions of STEM organizations and cultures include phrases such as "largely white, male dominated, anti-social, individualistic, and competitive" (Wentling & Thomas 2009, 27). The most frequently named cultural characteristic impeding women's career progress was the "male dominated, old boy" nature of the culture (Wentling & Thomas 2009, 31). The literature regarding the career advancement barriers reported most frequently by women included the lack of acceptance of women in a masculine STEM culture, isolation, and an old boys' network (Ceci & Williams 2010; Garcia-Retamero & Lopez-Zafra 2006; Hewlett et al. 2008; Hill et al. 2010; Page, Bailey, & VanDelinder 2009).

All sixteen participants in this study recounted experiences that illustrated the inequality regimes based on gender schema that are prevalent in gendered organizations. Participants described incidents in which men in positions of power invited aspiring men to participate in social activities that established relationships that were helpful when seeking career advancement but that women were excluded from activities in which career opportunities were often created.

Structural synthesis of theme 8: "You don't belong here; you are unwelcome here." Male-dominated STEM organizations tend to be gendered in nature and create inhospitable environments for women. Women were excluded from social activities that would be career enhancing. There is a perception among women in STEM that the power in their organizations resides in the "men's club" from which they are excluded based on their gender. Unlike the commonly held stereotype that women will compete with and undermine other women, the participants in this study found that the networks of other women in STEM were a source of great support, encouragement, organizational intelligence, and knowledge.

Both the deliberate and the unintended exclusion of women was prevalent in STEM organizations, and women viewed this as a major barrier for becoming known and gaining needed visibility for their talent and capabilities. However, these women remained focused and goal directed and found other ways to achieve success. The next section on buffering behaviors provides examples and descriptions of these other ways.

Buffering Behaviors: Four Themes

The first four elements of the conceptual framework describe the organizational challenges confronting many women and include (a) the generally held belief that leadership is a masculine domain, (b) the gender stereotypes that lead to bias, (c) gender backlash women encounter when they behave counterstereotypically, and (d) the gendered nature of many STEM organizations. Yet, there are women who persist, persevere, and succeed in reaching senior levels of leadership in STEM professions. The women in this study demonstrated resiliency, tenacity, and courage.

The expression *positive deviant* captures a key differentiating characteristic of the women who overcome gender-based barriers to achieve success in male-dominated STEM professions. A positive deviant is someone who faces the same challenges and obstacles as others in an organization but discovers "new and innovative ways to function without creating conflict" and who "systematically out performs others" (Allio 2011, 32–35). A person who exhibits positive deviance behaves in nonnormative ways in order to pursue honorable intentions (Appelbaum,

Iaconi, Matousek 2007; Pascale, Sternin, & Sternin 2010).). The last element of the conceptual framework examines buffering behaviors and the role they may play in the lives of women who have overcome gender-based barriers and challenges.

Recent studies have shown that certain buffering behaviors enable many self-efficacious women to overcome the gender-based challenges they often encounter as they seek to attain senior leadership roles in STEM organizations (Cech, Rubineau, Silbey, & Seron 2011; Gupta 2013; Jalbert, Jalbert, & Furumo 2013; O'Neill & O'Reilly 2011; Shaughnessy et al. 2011; Todd, Harris, Harris, & Wheeler 2009). These buffering behaviors include, but are not limited to, self-monitoring (Bandura 2001; Gupta 2013; O'Neill & O'Reilly 2011), impression management (Hirshfield 2011; O'Neill & O'Reilly 2011; Singh, Kumra, & Vinnicombe 2002), political skill (Shaughnessy, Treadway, Breland, Williams, & Brouer 2011; Todd, Harris, Harris, & Wheeler 2009), and performance (Jalbert, Jalbert, & Furumo 2013).

Buffering behavior theme 9: "Be alert and self-aware." Self-monitoring is a behavioral technique in which people assess and adjust their behavior within interpersonal and organizational situations and appears to be an effective buffering strategy for overcoming gender bias and backlash (Flynn & Ames 2006; Rudman & Phelan 2008; Shivers-Blackwell 2006).

People who self-monitor closely observe social cues and use this information to guide their behavior, which is particularly helpful to women in organizations where strong gender norms exist (O'Neill & O'Reilly 2011). Studies have shown that self-monitoring has a positive effect on promotions, interview success, and performance ratings (Flynn & Ames 2006; O'Neill & O'Reilly 2011). In studies of work groups consisting of both men and women, women who were high self-monitors were rated as more influential and more likely to emerge as leaders in the group than men and women who were low self-monitors (Shivers-Blackwell 2006). Studies have also shown that self-monitoring is effective in overcoming negative gender stereotypes (Flynn & Ames 2006). Self-monitoring is a particularly effective variable in a nontraditional leader's success (Anderson & Thacker 1985).

The women in this study reported that self-monitoring, an important buffering behavior for women in STEM, required that they continually exercise heightened levels of self-awareness and self-analysis. By carefully observing the effect of their words and actions on others, women created a convention of successful behaviors that guided them as they advanced in their careers. The women in this study all reported the importance of self-monitoring and developing a continual state of consciousness of any behaviors or language that might set them apart in a negative way. Maintaining this constant state of vigilance permeated the daily routine of the women in the study. Alice stated, "It's something you have to be aware of every day: what you wear to work, how you present—you have to engineer this thing."

Structural synthesis of theme 9: "Self-monitoring—be alert and self-aware." Self-monitoring, an important buffering behavior for women in STEM, required that women continuously exercise heightened levels of self-awareness and self-analysis. However, participants felt that it was an unfair gender-based burden in STEM and that the energy they expended on constant self-monitoring could have been better used elsewhere. Several observed that the expectations regarding what they wear, how they stand, where they sit, how they sound, what they say, with whom they socialize, are inconsistent, unpredictable, and unclear. What is acceptable for the men in the organization is not always acceptable for women. The dilemma is learning what the rules are because they fall within the category of tacit knowledge—unwritten, unspoken, and generally known by some and not others.

Buffering behavior theme 10: "Analyze, evaluate, adjust your behavior." Self-monitoring is especially pertinent to the study of buffering behaviors because it provides a framework within which individuals formulate behaviors and actions that create positive public impressions.

Those who actively self-monitor are more likely to utilize also the buffering behavior of impression management (Gangestad and Snyder 2000).

Impression management, also known as self-presentation, is a conscious process by which individuals seek to create a specific impression on others to elicit certain reactions (Guadagno & Cialdini 2007; Singh, Kumra, & Vinnicombe 2002). Goffman (1959) introduced the concept of impression management and observed that "it is in an individuals' best interests to influence other people's perceptions of themselves in order to control others' conduct and reactions to them" (p. 6) He noted that one's choice of actions could influence the outcomes of a situation (Goffman 1959). Women in STEM professions are often viewed as less expert than their male counterparts (Singh, Kumra, & Vinnicombe 2002) and the impression management technique of self-promotion has been used effectively to counteract those perceptions (Gilrane 2013). Gardner and Martinko (1988) linked Goffman's impression management (IM) theory (1959) to organizational theory and posited, "IM behaviors are potentially related to individual success and promotability within organizations" (p. 321).

The buffering behavior of impression management played a major role in the behavioral template used by the women in this study. They reported being constantly aware of specific behavior choices such as appearance, semantics, group affiliations, and meeting behavior. Five subcategories of impression management emerged from the data: (a) executive appearance, (b) communication and language choices, (c) associations, (d) adapting and adjusting, and (e) differentiating yourself.

All sixteen of the participants reported extensive use of impression management behaviors including adopting an executive appearance, being conscious of communication and language choices, taking care to associate and affiliate appropriately, being flexible in order to constantly adapt and adjust, and differentiate oneself.

Participants reported exercising great care and forethought when formulating statements and answering questions to ensure that their language choices strengthened rather than minimized their power. The women also described the need for extreme tact when challenging a colleague's conclusion or interpretation of a scientific or engineering problem.

Three of the women in the study suggested that it was important to be cautious about explanations regarding home-related issues that might be viewed through a negatively tinted gender lens. The women agreed that offering a child-care reason for not attending a meeting was viewed differently and negatively when it came from a woman but positively when it came from a man. Three of the participants, all from different STEM fields, stated that the groups with which one chooses to affiliate played a part in impression management. Gender-based stereotypes were important to recognize and to avoid.

Structural synthesis of theme 10: impression management—"Analyze, evaluate, adjust your behaviors." All sixteen of the participants reported extensive use of impression management behaviors including adopting an executive appearance, being conscious of communication and language choices, taking care to associate and affiliate appropriately, being flexible in order to constantly adapt and adjust, and differentiating oneself. Many of the women observed that the imperative to adapt and adjust behavior appeared to fall within the domain of the women in STEM and not the men. While they recognized this as unfair, they did not allow these disparate expectations to stall their forward progress. Yasmin, an engineer, described this distinct difference in the following observation: "When you work with a bunch of men, you have to adapt. It's not fair because why don't they adapt, right? But it's fine, it can be done. They may not know how to talk to me, but I can learn how to talk to them. So that's what I've done, is adapt, and then you change your behavior. And eventually, that pays off."

Sabine added, "I will admit that I have used my height and stature in ways to assert myself. You need to use the tools that you have. The more important the meeting, the higher the heels. I try to make myself a presence."

The energy that the women in the study devoted to impression management was significant, and all participants listed this as an important competency of which women who seek leadership in male-dominated field must be aware.

Buffering behavior theme 11: "Develop skills in networking, negotiating, communicating, and interpersonal savvy." Organizations are political in nature, and career advancement is frequently associated with politically astute behavior (Mintzberg 1985). Politically effective behavior is "the ability to effectively understand others at work and to use such knowledge to influence others to act in ways that enhance one's personal and/or organizational objectives" (Ferris, Treadway, Kolodinsky, Hochwarter, Kacmar, Douglas, & Frink 2005, 127). Political skill in this study falls within the category of social effectiveness and includes the constructs of social intelligence, social skill, and social competence (Ferris et al. 2007). Five subcategories of political skill emerged from the data: (a) visibility and networking, (b) negotiating, (c) crafting communications, (d) interpersonal savvy, and (e) empathy. Political skill is a broad set of competencies and includes, but is not limited to, "interpersonal acumen, sociopolitical intelligence, functional flexibility, social intelligence, and interpersonal intelligence" (Ferris et al. 2007).

The women in this study frequently mentioned the importance of positive visibility within the organization to career growth. Participants agreed that seizing opportunities to speak, to head initiatives, and to participate in activities in which senior leaders were involved created visibility opportunities. Often, the networks that women created became significant sources for career advancement.

Participants named negotiating skills as a subset of political skills and gave examples of how critically important these skills were to accomplishing desired outcomes. Negotiating skills utilized were both internally within the organization and externally with clients and partners.

The women in this study defined political behavior broadly and included the ability to read others and shift their behavior accordingly. All of the women in the study were familiar with their Myers Briggs Type Indicator® preferences. They discussed knowing and using the communication and influencing approaches that were most effective with people whose MBTI preferences were different from their own.

Participants reported that the knowledge and use of interpersonal skills (i.e., insight into human needs, collaboration, use of positive and appreciative feedback, nonadversarial approaches, and humor) were extremely important to their ability to accomplish goals and achieve senior leadership roles. Participants also indicated that an awareness of the needs, feelings, and perspectives of others was an important aspect of political skill. Studies of emotional intelligence in leadership, authentic leadership, and charismatic leadership all cite the role of empathy as a critical success factor (Kellett 2002).

Structural synthesis of theme 11: "Develop skills in networking, negotiating, communicating, and interpersonal savvy." Women discovered and developed several essential skills to navigate successfully the political landscape of their STEM organizations. These skills included the ability to negotiate and achieve desired outcomes, to create networks among the power brokers, to learn to communicate in the "language of the land," and to use empathy to develop high levels of interpersonal insight and savvy. Many women viewed their political skill and interpersonal competency as a gendered advantage over their less interpersonally adept male colleagues in STEM, who are mainly scientists, technologists, engineers, and mathematicians. Instead of being deterred by the gender-based obstacles they encountered, the women in this study used highly developed interpersonal and political skills to navigate around the barriers. When negotiating with a competing peer to hire a biologist for her team, Claire explained, "I got what I wanted, by not confronting him, but by acknowledging his ego, his empire, his territory. By making some nonmaterial concessions, I got what I wanted. I hadn't thought about what I did with the biologist hire as a mitigating behavior. But it certainly was."

Buffering behavior theme 12: "You can't be equal to, you must be better than. You must overprepare, overachieve, overdeliver." In a study of success factors of women leaders in engineering, nine out of the 10 women participants stated that going above and beyond their job duties, excelling in their assignments and working long hours and sometimes weekends were all strategies that enabled them to move ahead in their careers (Jepson 2010, 88). In another study of 158 managers in organizations, women credited hard work for their achievements rather than ability (Rosenthal 1995). High-ranking women in technology attribute their success to high levels of perseverance, persistence despite adversity or discouragement, and self-reliance (Borg 2010).

The findings in this study confirm those of similar studies in which women identified consistently overperforming and exceeding performance expectations as important career advancement strategies. Women in this study felt there was a definite gender disparity in the preconceived beliefs held about a woman's ability to perform in STEM, and they used intensive in-depth preparation, some called it overpreparation, to demonstrate their competency.

All sixteen of the women in this study identified exceptional performance, long hours, in-depth preparation, citing scientific sources to back up positions, and keen process analysis as important ways they achieved senior leadership. One participant summarized the views of others when she said, "You can't be equal to, you must be better than." The participants identified five subcategories of performance: (a) overpreparation, (b) availability, (c) exceeding expectations, (d) scientific knowledge, intellect, cognitive and analytical skills, and (e) being the intervening variable.

Women in the study encountered the supposition that women

with children would not be as available and/or dedicated as men. The women had to make it clear that they could travel at a moment's notice or be available to meet at night or on the weekends.

Participants provided specific examples of how exceeding performance expectations was an essential tool for overcoming gender-based perceptions and barriers. Women also mentioned that while excellent performance was a positive differentiator, it had to be done with finesse.

Several of the women in the study cited the importance of scientific, technical, and process knowledge as a differentiating quality. Participants gave numerous examples of how the ability to assess and analyze a situation and then provide accurate diagnoses and/or workable solutions resulted in creating a perception of being an asset to the organization.

Participants mentioned that it was important to be recognized as someone who identifies and takes on projects that are in trouble and then turns them around, to be the individual who steps in to solve problems that have caused a project or a team to become delayed, and/or to be someone who uses her particular talents in a way that becomes the intervening variable to the success of a project. As such, being in a lead contributor role rather than in a support role was important.

Structural synthesis of theme 12: "You can't be equal to, you must be better than. You must overprepare, overachieve, overdeliver." Of all the buffering behaviors discussed and employed by the women in this study, performance in the form of superlative achievement, intense preparation, and exceptional results was most often cited and most often credited for women's success in STEM. The participants came to work early, they stayed late, and they worked on the weekends. Not only did they spend more time on the job, they used this time to prepare thoroughly and to ensure that they left very little to chance. The participants reported that they felt there was definitely a performance double standard in which men would be more easily forgiven a misstatement or an oversight of data, but this behavior on the part of a woman would be used to confirm the hypothesis that they didn't' have what it took to succeed in a demanding field such as STEM. Kate's lived experience provides a compelling glimpse of the hard work required, the gender disparity of expectations, and the unrelenting nature of the requirement to overprepare, overachieve, overdeliver.

> If I get up there on the stage, and I'm not prepared, I'm a dumb broad. I think you have to work harder, no doubt. I think you have to be technically better. I think you have to do it in the absence of benefiting from the old boys' network, since there is no girls' network, not really. Just have the facts. Do your research; just make sure you're on top of the game. That's the difference between a man and a woman; you have to prove yourself more. It's constant; it never ends. And sometimes it's exhausting.

Strengths and Limitations

Strengths

The compelling stories shared by the study participants and the powerful insights they revealed represent the greatest strengths of the study. For other women who are struggling to overcome gender-based barriers, this data provides specific behavioral strategies and approaches to utilize when encountering gender-based discrimination. Another strength of this study is the feminist theory framework, which ensures that women's viewpoints, experiences, and perspectives are equally valued and reflected (Brooks & Hesse-Biber 2007; Landman 2006). This methodology placed women at the center of the study rather than as subjects to be studied. Feminist research tenets seek to ensure that research (a) is focused on the social realities of women, (b) informs policies, practices, and decisions that are fair and inclusive (c) utilizes a collaborative model of inquiry between the participant and the researcher, and (d) eliminates existing stereotypes (Landman 2006).

Many of the participants reported that the retelling of these experiences was cathartic and therapeutic. Upon reading the transcripts of their interviews, participants expressed renewed commitment to provide guidance to other women, especially junior staff, as they confront gender-based barriers in STEM.

Limitations

The study is limited to women who have attained senior leadership positions in fields of science, technology, engineering, and mathematics. Women in other professions or at entry-level or midlevel management were included in the study, and this may limit the generalization of the results. Including only those women who have already achieved senior executive status might exclude points of view not shared by women who have not broken through the glass ceiling. The participants were selected on the basis of agreeing to be interviewed and may be seen as a convenience sample, inadvertently excluding participants with differing points of view. The participants were all from North American organizations, primarily in the northeastern United States, and it is acknowledged that cultural norms regarding gender differ in other parts of the world. These differences in cross-cultural gender norms may also limit the transferability of findings to other cultural populations. However, the reader will be the best judge of the transferability of the findings, and it is hoped that the rich, thick descriptions of the themes and phenomena will assist in this determination.

Conclusions and Implications

One of the most important conclusions of this study was the critical role of highly developed beliefs of self-efficacy as a foundational element for all the women in this study. Important developmental sources of self-efficacy included early messages from parents and teachers and early experiences of responsibility. A surprising and often cited source of self-efficacy for the women in the study was the opportunity to compete in athletics or physical challenges such as Outward Bound.

Another aspect of self-efficacy was the use of internal dialogue. When women experienced self-doubt, they utilized positive self-talk, and many had scripts that they repeated as if they were mantras. As scientists, they used evidence and data to refute flawed hypotheses about their performance capabilities.

The study also found that discovering that they had alternatives and did not have to stay in untenable situations was a source of power for the participants. Women recognized that very few would be championed for leadership roles the way their male colleagues were, so they had to take control of their own career destinies.

Masculine hegemony and the inhospitable gendered environments found in STEM organizations led to widespread incidents of sexual harassment and sexual discrimination. Every woman in the study reported experiencing gender-based discriminatory behaviors, beliefs, decisions, and actions and that it caught them by surprise. An interesting common denominator was that none of the women filed charges of sexual harassment or unfair labor practices, nor did they seek third-party interventions from Human Resources or external regulatory agencies. They stated that they had consciously chosen to compete on a male-dominated playing field and that they would find or develop ways to succeed without asking for third-party interventions.

The women in this study all exhibited behaviors consistent with the concept of positive deviance. The term *positive deviant* is used to describe people who "with exactly the same resources and circumstances as everyone else, are consistently and significantly more successful than the norm (Pascale, Sternin, & Sternin 2010).

The development and use of buffering behaviors by the study

participants represents positive deviance in that they encountered widespread incidents of gender bias and discrimination in STEM education and organizations but did not leave the field as many have (leaky pipeline). Instead, they developed and used strategies and behaviors that resulted in consistent and significant experiences of success.

Implications for Women in STEM

This study shows strategies and behaviors exist that women in STEM can utilize to overcome the pervasive gender-based barriers to leadership frequently encountered in the fields of science, technology, engineering, and mathematics. Foundational to one's ability to apply these mitigating mechanisms known as buffering behaviors is a strong sense of self-efficacy, which developed for the women in this study early in life. The implications of these findings suggest that in addition to providing access and encouragement for young girls to study science, technology, engineering, and mathematics, messages and experiences that develop self-efficacy are essential. In addition to affirming messages from significant adults in their lives, successful women leaders in STEM said athletic competition, physical challenges, and having responsibilities early in life built self-efficacious beliefs. The practice of using encouraging internal dialogue known as positive self-talk is another skill set women who seek leadership in STEM need to develop.

When beliefs of self-efficacy are deep and strong, women are then more likely to develop and utilize the buffering behaviors identified by the women in this study. The importance of self-monitoring, impression management, political skill, and performance need to be incorporated into the curriculum. Skills identified as important in impression management included (a) executive appearance, (b) communication and language choices, (c) associations, (d) adapting and adjusting, and (e) differentiating yourself. Political skills included the ability to negotiate and achieve desired outcomes, to create networks among power brokers, to communicate in the "language of the land," and to use empathy to develop high levels of interpersonal insight and savvy. Women must understand that exceptional performance is prerequisite to the use of any of the other buffering behaviors. It is also important for them to recognize and accept that in order for their performance to be viewed as exceptional, they will likely have to overprepare, overachieve, and overdeliver.

Implications for STEM Organizations

Organizations that do not utilize the talent of both men and women are not realizing optimal value or leveraging the full range of resources available. Extensive research shows that diversity is necessary and valuable, and yet STEM organizations continue to lack diversity, especially in the senior ranks of leadership. As a result, teams that lack heterogeneity risk group think, limited views, and flawed designs.

By bringing to light leadership inequities and the potential exclusion of talented individuals, the researcher hopes that organizations and leaders will assist more women in breaking through the barriers that block their upward progress. Discovering and making known the strategies that have enabled some women to overcome gender-based barriers and hold leadership positions may also empower other women in male-dominated professions to strive for similar success.

Recommendations for Future Research

In the course of this study, a number of additional issues surfaced that would be important to investigate in more depth. One would be the role of unconscious bias and how pervasive this is in organizations that claim to be models of equal opportunity. Mental models of leadership, autonomy and relational skills, are worthy of further exploration.

There still exist deep pockets of misogyny that warrant exploration.

What is the source? Can one's views change? As Virginia Wolf wrote in *A Room of One's Own* (1945), "The history of men's opposition to women's emancipation is more interesting perhaps than the story of that emancipation itself." Another research suggestion would be to design a study that examines the views of men in senior STEM positions who are promoting and hiring women into leadership roles. What are the qualities and criteria they are using to make these selections? Are there common characteristics among the men who promote women? Are men with daughters more likely or less likely to champion women for leadership roles in STEM? Are political, philosophical, or religious views regarding the place of women significant? How can and do men become aware of unconscious bias?

The women in this study were exemplars of an internal locus of control orientation. Instead of focusing on the external organizational and structural barriers to advancement using an external locus of control interpretation of the environment, they empowered themselves to achieve their desired outcomes employing an internal locus of control lens. A potential area of inquiry would be to explore the spectrum of internal/external locus of control perceptions of aspiring women leaders.

Reflections

Recalling and recounting the extent of the gender bias they encountered was an emotionally raw experience for the participants, and many said the memory of the mistreatment was so vivid it felt as though it happened yesterday. The aftereffects still lingered for many of the participants. These incidents of gender discrimination happened to many of these women when they were young, inexperienced, and vulnerable. The impact of these experiences was profound and lasting, and the emotional content expressed when recounting these incidents was deep and reflected hurt and pain.

They did not seek external interventions but instead took it upon themselves to find ways to overcome the inequities and the ill treatment. They did not forget these early experiences and reached out to young women to guide and support them as they entered STEM organizations. An important finding of the study refutes the generally held stereotype that women often treat other women unfairly. The preponderance of women in this study reported that they both provided and received support, encouragement, and mentoring from other women.

The amazing choice to channel the anger and resentment into proactive success strategies provides important lessons to other women who are experiencing gender-based discrimination. We may not have control over the situations in which we find ourselves, but we do have control over our reactions and behaviors to these situations. These successful women did not spend time perseverating or remaining stuck in recriminations. Nor did they file charges although the discriminatory treatment and circumstances warranted it on many occasions. Instead, they chose to persevere toward their goals and found ways around, over, under, and through.

Many of the women upon reading the transcript of the session called to say how therapeutic the experience had been and how it put things in perspective for them. The pervasiveness of male hegemony was a source of disillusionment to many of the women when their male colleagues observed inappropriate and unfair treatment and said nothing. Women concluded they would have to make their way alone.

Buffering Behaviors

In the face of the persistent and, at times, pernicious gender bias and discrimination, women developed a range of behaviors that mitigated the impact of the unequal, inequitable, unfair treatment they encountered. The most prevalent of these buffering behaviors was performance. The findings of this study confirmed earlier studies in which women reported the importance of overperforming and exceeding performance expectations as important career advancement strategies. Many of the participants observed that intelligence and innovative problem solving were competitive advantages in STEM professions. All sixteen participants referenced their ability to deliver superior work, solve complex problems, and offer important insights. They also reported working extraordinary hours, preparing extensively, being uberprepared. They agreed that hard work and long hours were necessary but not sufficient to succeed—that one must also deliver exceptional results. These successful women leaders in STEM organizations are exceptionally bright and capable. They used their intelligence and scientific training to analyze the hostile situations in which they found themselves, identified possible solutions, and experimented with responses and solutions. Many actually created behavioral matrixes of successful behavioral solutions to a variety of people and situations.

The title of this dissertation, "Solving for X in the Y Domain," came from the lived experiences of the participants to view the challenges they faced in much the same way as they viewed scientific, technological, engineering, or mathematical problems. They frequently used the expression "solve for X" to describe how they thought about challenging situations.

Summary

This study explored the phenomenon addressed in the central research question: What are the lived experiences of women in STEM senior leadership using buffering behaviors to overcome gender bias and achieve success? All sixteen participants reported encountering discriminatory and hostile gender-based treatment in STEM. These successful women, all of whom hold senior leadership positions in STEM, are distinguished by their highly developed sense of self-efficacy. As a result, when dealing with mistreatment, they demonstrated resiliency, tenacity, and courage. The development and use of buffering behaviors (self-monitoring, impression management, political skill, and performance) was instrumental in mitigating the gender-based hostility and was a shared success strategy.

> Life is not easy for any of us. But what of that? We must have perseverance and above all confidence in ourselves. We must believe that we are gifted for something and that this thing must be attained.
>
> —Madame Curie

REFERENCES

Acker, J. (2006). "Inequality regimes: Gender, class, and race in organizations." *Gender & Society* 20, 441–64. Retrieved from http://gas.sagepub.com/cgi/content/abstract/20/4/441.

Adler, R. D. (2001). "Women in the executive suite correlate to high profits." *Harvard Business Review* 79(3). Retrieved from http://www.w2t.se/se/filer/adler_web.pdf.

Adler, R. D. (2009). "Profit thy name is woman?" *Pacific Standard*. Retrieved from http://www.psmag.com/business-economics/profit-thy-name-is-woman–3920/.

Allio, R. J. (2011). "How corporate leaders can use the positive deviance approach to stimulate radical change." *Strategy & Leadership 39*(3), 32–35. http://dx.doi.org/10.1108/10878571111128793.

Anderson, R. (2007). "Thematic content analysis: Descriptive presentation of qualitative data." Retrieved from Wellknowing Consulting Services website: http://www.wellknowingconsulting.org/publications/pdfs/ThematicContentAnalysis.pdf.

Appelbaum, S. H., G. D. Iaconi, & A. Matousek. (2007). "Positive and negative deviant workplace behaviors: Causes, impacts, and solutions." *Corporate Governance 7*(5), 586–98. http://dx.doi.org/10.1108/14720700710827176.

Arp, K. (2000). "A different voice in the phenomenological tradition: Simone de Beauvoir and the ethic of care." In L. Fisher & L. Embree (eds.), *Feminist phenomenology*, 71–81. Dordrecht, Netherlands: Kluwer Academic.

Atkinson, P., A. Coffey, S. Delamont, & M. Hammersly. (2005). "Key themes in qualitative research: Continuities and change." *British Educational Research Journal 31*(3), 405–8. Retrieved from http://www.jstor.org/stable/30032633 10.2307/30032633.

Babcock, L., & S. Laschever. (2003). *Women don't ask. Negotiation and the Gender Divide.* Princeton, NJ: Princeton University Press. Retrieved from http://hbr.org/2003/10/nice-girls-dont-ask/.

Bailey, J. (2008). "First steps in qualitative data analysis: Transcribing." *Family Practice 25*, 127–31. Retrieved from http://web.mit.edu/ombuds/publications/barriers.pdf.

Bandura, A. (1994). "Self-efficacy." In V. S. Ramachaudran (ed.), *Encyclopedia of Human Behavior* 4, 71–81. New York: Academic Press. Retrieved from http://www.westga.edu/~vickir/Healthcare/HC14%20FacititatingResiliency/Link%2010%20--%20Self-Efficacy.pdf.

Bandura, A. (2001). "Social cognitive theory: An agentic perspective." *Annual Review of Psychology* 52, 1–26. Retrieved from www.annualreviews.org.

Bandura, A., G. V. Caprara, C. Barbaranelli, M. Gerbino, & C. Pastorelli. (2003). "Role of affective self-regulatory efficacy in diverse spheres of psychosocial functioning." *Child Development 74*(3), 769–82. Retrieved from http://www.uky.edu/~eushe2/BanduraPubs/BanduraEtAlCD2003.pdf.

Barkacs, L. L., & S. Standifird. (2008). "Gender distinctions and empathy in negotiation." *Journal of Organizational Culture, Communication and Conflict 12*(1), 83–92. Retrieved from http://search.proquest.com/docview/216602862?accountid=34120.

Barker, L., C. Mancha, & C. Ashcraft. (2014). *What is the impact of gender diversity on technology business performance? Research summary.* Retrieved from National Center for Women & Information Technology website: http://www.ncwit.org/sites/default/files/resources/impactgenderdiversitytechbusinessperformance_print.pdf.

Barreto, M. E., M. K. Ryan, & M. T. Schmitt. (2009). *The glass ceiling in the 21st century: Understanding barriers to gender equality*. Washington, DC: American Psychological Association.

Barsh, J., & L. Yee. (2011). *Unlocking the full potential of women in the U.S. economy*. Retrieved from McKinsey and Company website: http://www.mckinsey.com/client_service/organization/latest_thinking/unlocking_the_full_potential.

Basit, T. N. (2003). "Manual or electronic? The role of coding in qualitative data analysis." *Educational Researc*, 45(2), 143–54. http://dx.doi.org/10.1080/0013188032000103235.

Bell, A. A. (2010). "A phenomenological inquiry of women's lived experiences in preparing for high-level leadership positions" (doctoral dissertation). Available from ProQuest Dissertations and Theses database. (AAT: 3407434).

Berry, P., & T. J. Franks. (2010). "Women in the world of corporate business: Looking at the glass ceiling." *Contemporary Issues in Education Research* 3(2), 1–9. Retrieved from http://www.cluteinstitute.com/ojs/index.php/CIER/article/view/171.

Borg, Anita Institute. "Top six attributes of high-ranking women in technology." (2010). *Health & Beauty Close-Up*. Retrieved from http://search.proquest.com/docview/818856985?accountid=34120.

Borgatta, E. F., R. F. Bales, & A. S. Couch. (1954). "Some findings relevant to the great man theory of leadership." *American Sociological Review* 19(6), 755–59. Retrieved from http://www.jstor.org/discover/10.2307/2087923?uid=3739600&uid=2&uid=4&uid=3739256&sid=21103658235301.

Bowles, H. R. (2012). "Claiming authority: How women explain their ascent to top business leadership positions." *Research in Organizational Behavior* 32, 189–212. Retrieved from http://web.hks.harvard.edu/publications/workingpapers/citation.aspx?PubId=8639.

Brannstrom, I. A. (2004). "Gender stratification in management: The World Health Organization 2000." *Journal of Health Organization and Management* 18(1), 7–15. Retrieved from http://www.ncbi. nlm.nih.gov/pubmed/15133880.

Brescoll, V. L., E. Dawson, & E. L. Uhlmann. (2010). "Hard won and easily lost: The fragile status of leaders in gender-stereotype-incongruent occupations." *Association for Psychological Science* 22, 1–3. http://dx.doi.org/10.1177/0956797610384744.

Brooks, A., & S. N. Hesse-Biber. (2007). "An invitation to feminist research." In *Feminist research practice: A primer*, 1–24. Retrieved from http://www.onlinecef.net./file.php/1/CEF_Resources/ Research%20%20Method/12935_Chapter1.pdf.

Bruckmüller, S., & N. R. Branscombe. (2011, January–February). "How women end up on the 'glass cliff.'" *Harvard Business Review*. Retrieved from http://hbr.org/2011/01/ how-women-end-up-on-the-glass-cliff.

Buck Luce, C., S. A. Hewlett, L. J. Servon, L. Sherbin, P. Shiller, E. Sosnovich, & K. Sumberg. (2008). "The Athena factor: Reversing the brain drain in science." Retrieved from http://documents. library.nsf.gov/edocs/HD6060-.A84-2008-PDF-Athena-facto r-Reversing-the-brain-drain-in-science,-engineering,-and-technology.pdf.

Bureau of Labor Statistics, US Department of Labor. (2012). *Labor force statistics from the Current Population Survey*. Retrieved from Bureau of Labor Statistics website: http://www.bls.gov/cps/ lfcharacteristics.htm.

Burnard, P. (1994). "Searching for meaning: A method of analysing interview transcripts with a personal computer." *Nurse Education Today* 14, 111–17. Retrieved from http://www.acrn.eu/cambridge/ downloads/files/sample_coding.pdf.

Bussey, K., & A. Bandura. (1999). "Social cognitive theory of gender development and differentiation." *Psychological Review* 106,

676–713. Retrieved from http://jpkc.ecnu.edu.cn/fzxlx/jiaoxue/Social%20Cognitive%20Theory%20of%20Gender%20Development%20and%20Differentiation.pdf.

Catalyst. (2003). *Bit by bit: Catalyst's guide to women in high-tech companies.* Retrieved from Catalyst website: http://www.catalyst.org/knowledge/bit-bit-catalyst-guide-advancing-women-high-tech-companies.

Catalyst. (2011). *The bottom line: Corporate performance and women's representation on boards (2004–2008).* Retrieved from Catalyst website: http://www.catalyst.org/knowledge/bottom-line-corporate-performance-and-womens-representation-boards-20042008.

Catalyst. (2012). *Why diversity matters.* Retrieved from Catalyst website: http://www.catalyst.org/knowledge/why-diversity-matters.

Catalyst. (2013). *Catalyst quick take: Statistical overview of women in the workplace.* Retrieved from Catalyst website: http://www.catalyst.org/knowledge/statistical-overview-women-workplace.

Catalyst. (2014). *Women CEOs of the Fortune 1000.* Retrieved from Catalyst website: http://www.catalyst.org/knowledge/women-ceos-fortune–1000.

Cech, E., B. Rubineau,, S. Silbey, & C. Seron. (2011). "Professional role confidence and gendered persistence in engineering." *American Sociological Review* 76(5), 641–66. Retrieved from http://search.proquest.com/docview/901614929?accountid=34120.

Ceci, S. J., & W. M. Williams. (2010). "Understanding current causes of women's underrepresentation in science." *Proceedings of the National Academy of Sciences* 108(8), 3157–162. Retrieved from http://www.pnas.org/content/108/8/3157.full.

Chen, C. P. (2006). "Strengthening career human agency." *Journal of Counseling and Development* 84(2), 131–38. http://dx.doi.org/10.1002/j.1556-6678.2006.tb00388.x.

Chen, Z., K. Roy, & C. A. G. Crawford, (2010). "Examining the role of gender in career advancement at the centers for disease control and prevention." *American Journal of Public Health* 100(3), 426-34. Retrieved from http://search.proquest.com/docview/215084882?accountid=34120.

Clark, K. E. (2005). "Why some women leave corporate leadership positions and why other women remain: A phenomenological study" (doctoral dissertation). Available from ProQuest Dissertations and Theses database. (UMI No. X).

Cole, A. R. (2014). *Sports participation and academic achievement: Does self-efficacy play a role?* Available from ProQuest Dissertations & Theses Database. (UMI No. 1532772157).

Connell, R. W., & J. W. Messerschmidt. (2005). "Hegemonic masculinity: Rethinking the concept." *Gender & Society* 19(6), 829–59. http://dx.doi.org/10.1177/0891243205278639.

Cooper, R. (2009). "Decoding coding via *The Coding Manual for Qualitative Researchers* by Johnny Saldaña." *Weekly Qualitative Report* 2(42), 245–48. Retrieved from http://www.nova.edu/ssss/QR/WQR/saldana.pdf.

Cotter, D. A., J. M. Hermsen, S. Ovadia, & R. Vanneman. (2001). "The glass ceiling effect." *Social Forces* 80(2), 655–82. Retrieved from http://www.vanneman.umd.edu/papers/CotterHOV01.pdf.

Creswell, J. W. (2013). *Qualitative inquiry and research design: Choosing among five approaches* (3rd ed.). Thousand Oaks, CA: Sage.

Crosby, F., C. Clayton, O. Alksnis, & K. Hemker. (1986). "Cognitive biases in the perception of discrimination: The importance of format." *Sex Roles* 14(11–12), 637–46. http://dx.doi.org/10.1007/BF00287694.

D'Agostino, M., & H. Levine. (2009). "The career progression of women in state government agencies." *Gender in Management: An International Journal* 25(1), 22–36. http://dx.doi.org/10.1108/17542411011019913.

De Castro, A. (2003). "Introduction to Giorgi's existential phenomenological research method." *Psicología desde el Caribe*. 11, 45–56. Retrieved from http://rcientificas.uninorte.edu.co/index. php/psicologia/article/viewFile/1717/1112.

DeGroot, C., A. Mohapatra, & J. Lippmann. (2013). "Examining the cracks in the ceiling: A survey of corporate diversity practices of the S&P 100." *Calvert Diversity Report*. Retrieved from http:// www.calvert.com/nrc/literature/documents/BR10063.pdf.

Dencker, J. C. (2008). "Corporate restructuring and sex differences in managerial promotion." *American Sociological Review* 73(3), 455–76. http://dx.doi.org/10.1177/000312240807300305.

DeVault, M. L. (1996). "Talking back to sociology: Distinctive contributions of feminist methodology." *Annual Review of Sociology* 22, 29–50. Retrieved from http://cooley.libarts.wsu.edu/schwartj/ pdf/FemMethod.pdf.

Desvaux, G., S. Devillard, & S. Sancier-Sultan. (2010). *Women at the top of corporations: Making it happen.* Retrieved from http://www. mckinsey.com/features/women_matter.

Dezsö, C. L., & D. G. Ross. (2012). "Does female representation in top management improve firm performance? A panel data investigation." *Strategic Management Journal* 33(9), 1072–089. Retrieved from http://www8.gsb.columbia.edu/sites/ financialstudies/files/files/female_representation.pdf.

Donhoe, D. (2013). "The Definition of STEM?" Retrieved from http:// www.todaysengineer.org/2013/Dec/STEM-definition.asp

Drucker, P. F. (1939). *The end of economic man: A study of the new totalitarianism.* Retrieved from https://www. foreignaffairs.com/reviews/capsule-review/1939-10-01/ end-economic-man-study-new-totalitarianism.

———. (1995). *The future of industrial man* (vol. 1). Piscataway, NJ: Transaction.

Eagly, A. H., & S. J. Karau. (2002). "Role congruity theory of prejudice toward female leaders." *Psychological Review* 109(3), 573–98. Retrieved from http://psycnet.apa.org/journals/rev/109/3/573/.

Eagly, A. H., & L. L. Carli. (2003). "The female leadership advantage: An evaluation of the evidence." *Leadership Quarterly* 14(6), 807–34. http://dx.doi.org/10.1016/j.leaqua.2003.09.004.

Eagly, A. H., & W. Wood. (1991). "Explaining sex differences in social behavior: A meta-analytic perspective." *Personality and Social Psychology Bulletin* 17, 306–15. Retrieved from http://files.eric.ed.gov/fulltext/ED303721.pdf.

Ehrich, L. (2005). "Revisiting phenomenology: Its potential for management research." Paper presented at Challenges for organisations in global markets, British Academy of Management Conference, Oxford University, Oxford, England. Retrieved from http://eprints.qut.edu.au/2893/1/2893.pdf.

Eldridge, C. B., P. Park, A. Phillips, & E. Williams. (2007). "Executive women in finance." *CPA Journal* 77(1), 58–60. Retrieved from http://www.questia.com/magazine/1P3–1201516301/executive-women-in-finance.

Englander, M. (2012). "The interview: Data collection in descriptive phenomenological human scientific research." *Journal of Phenomenological Psychology* 43(1), 13. Retrieved from http://phenomenologyblog.com/wp-content/uploads/2012/04/Englander–2012-The-Interview-Data-Collection-in-Descriptive-Phenomenological-Human-Scientific-Research.pdf.

Erhardt, N. L., J. D. Werbel, & C. B. Shrader. (2003). "Board of director diversity and firm financial performance." *Corporate Governance: An International Review* 11(2), 102–111.

Evans, D. (2010). "Aspiring to leadership … a woman's world? An example of developments in France." *Cross Cultural Management* 17(4), 347–67. http://dx.doi.org/10.1108/13527601011086577.

Ferris, G. R., D. C. Treadway, R. W. Kolodinsky, W. A. Hochwarter, C. J. Kacmar, C. Douglas, & D. D. Frink. (2005). "Development and Validation of the Political Skill Inventory." *Journal of Management* 31(1), 126–52. Retrieved from http://www2.cob.ilstu.edu/mpdumler/M421/political%20skill%20inventory.pdf.

Feyerherm, A., & Y. H. Vick. (2005). "Generation X women in high technology: Overcoming gender and generational challenges to succeed in the corporate environment." *Career Development International* 10(3), 216–27. http://dx.doi.org/10.1108/13620430510598337.

Fink, A. (2005). *Conducting research literature reviews: From the Internet to paper* (2nd ed.). Thousand Oaks, CA: Sage.

Finlay, L. (2009). "Debating phenomenological research methods." *Phenomenology & Practice* 3(1), 6–25. Retrieved from https://ejournals.library.ualberta.ca/index.php/pandpr/article/view/19818/15336.

Fisher, L. (2000). "Phenomenology and feminism: Perspectives on their relation." In L. Fisher & L. Embree (eds.), *Feminist phenomenology*, 12–38. Dordrecht, Netherlands: Kluwer Academic. Retrieved from http://www.janushead.org/13–1/SimmsStawarska.pdf.

Flynn, F. J., & D. Ames. (2006). "What's good for the goose may not be good for the gander: The benefits of self-monitoring for men and women." *Journal of Applied Psychology* 91(2), 272–81. Retrieved from http://www.columbia.edu/~da358/publications/flynn_ames_selfmonitoring.pdf.

Fossey, F., C. Harvey, F. McDermott, & L. Davidson. (2002). "Understanding and evaluating qualitative research." *Australian and New Zealand Journal of Psychiatry* 36(6), 717–32. Retrieved from http://www.stes-apes.med.ulg.ac.be/Documents_electroniques/MET/MET-DON/ELE%20MET-DON%20A–8082.pdf.

Foucault, M. (1994). *The order of things: An archaeology of the human sciences.* New York: Vintage Books. Retrieved from http://www.

naturalthinker.net/trl/texts/Foucault,Michel/Foucault,%20
Michel%20-%20The%20Order%20of%20Things%20-%20
An%20Archaeology%20of%20the%20Human%20Sciences.pdf.

Fox, M. F., & C. Colatrella. (2006). "Participation, performance, and advancement of women in academic science and engineering: What is at issue and why." *Journal of Technology Transfer* 31(3), 377–86. http://dx.doi.org/10.1007/s10961-006-7209-x.

Gangestad, S. W., & M. Snyder. (2000). "Self-monitoring: Appraisal and reappraisal." *Psychological Bulletin* 126(4), 530–55.

Garcia-Retamero, R., & E. Lopez-Zafra. (2006). „Prejudice against women in male-congenial environments: Perceptions of gender role congruity in leadership." *Sex Roles* 55(1–2), 51–61. http://dx.doi.org/10.1007/s11199-006-9068-1.

Gardner, W. L., & M. J. Martinko. (1988). "Impression management in organizations." *Journal of Management* 14(2), 321–38. Retrieved from http://www.researchgate.net/profile/William_Gardner3/publication/235431601_Impression_management_in_organizations/links/00b7d52b4a489009bc000000.pdf.

Gentry, W. A., D. C. Gilmore, M. L. Shuffler, & J. Leslie. (2012). "Political skill as an indicator of promotability among multiple rater sources." *Journal of Organizational Behavior* 33(1), 89–104. http://dx.doi.org/10.1002/job.740.

Gibson, S. K., & L. A. Hanes. (2003). "The contribution of phenomenology to HRD research." *Human Resource Development Review* 2, 181–205. Retrieved from http://hrd.sagepub.com/content/2/2/181.short.

Gilrane, V. L. (2013). "Behavioral correlates of metastereotypes: The relationship between impression management and supervisor perceptions of women in STEM" (doctoral dissertation). Available from ProQuest Dissertations and Theses database. (AAT: 3562517).

Giorgi, A. (2009). *The descriptive phenomenological method in psychology: A modified Husserlian approach.* Pittsburgh: Duquesne University Press.

Glick, P., & S. T. Fiske. (2001). "An ambivalent alliance: Hostile and benevolent sexism as complementary justifications for gender inequality." *American Psychologist* 56(2), 109. Retrieved from https://wesfiles.wesleyan.edu/courses/PSYC–309-clwilkins/week9/Glick.%20Fiske.%202001.pdf.

Goffman, E. (2012). "The presentation of self in everyday life." *Contemporary Sociological Theory*, 46–61. Retrieved from http://www.public.iastate.edu/~carlos/607/readings/goffman.pdf.

Gould, D., & M. Weiss. (1981). "The effects of model similarity and model talk on self-efficacy and muscular endurance." *Journal of Sport Psychology* 3(1), 17–29. Retrieved from http://journals.humankinetics.com/AcuCustom/Sitename/Documents/DocumentItem/8536.pdf.

Goulding, C. (2005). "Grounded theory, ethnography, and phenomenology: A comparative analysis of three qualitative strategies for marketing research." *European Journal of Marketing* 39(3), 294–308. Retrieved from http://search.proquest.com/docview/237028636?accountid=34120.

Green, M. T., P. Duncan, C. Salter, & E. Chavez. (2012). "The educated worker: An empirical investigation of expectations of leadership." *Journal of Leadership, Accountability and Ethics* 9(6), 94–112. Retrieved from http://connection.ebscohost.com/c/articles/89879745/educated-worker-empirical-investigation-expectations-leadership.

Green, J., & N. Thorogood. (2013). *Qualitative methods for health research* (3rd ed.). Thousand Oaks, CA: Sage.

Groenewald, T. (2004). "A phenomenological research design illustrated." *International Journal of Qualitative Methods* 3(1). Article 4. Retrieved from http://www.ualberta.ca/~iiqm/backissues/3_1/pdf/groenewald.pdf.

Guadagno, R. E., & R. B. Cialdini. (2007). "Gender differences in impression management in organizations: A qualitative review." *Sex Roles* 56(7–8), 483–94. http://dx.doi.org/10.1007/s11199-007-9187-3.

Guba, E. G. (1990). *The paradigm dialog.* Newbury Park, CA: Sage. Retrieved from http://www.appstate.edu/~jacksonay/rcoe/guba.pdf.

Guba, E. G., & Y. S. Lincoln. (1994). "Competing paradigms in qualitative research." In N. K. Denzin & Y. S. Lincoln (eds.), *Handbook of Qualitative Research,* 105–17). Retrieved from https://www.uncg.edu/hdf/facultystaff/Tudge/Guba%20&%20Lincoln%201994.pdf.

Guest, G., A. Bunce, & L. Johnson. (2006). "How many interviews are enough? An experiment with data saturation and variability." *Field methods* 18(1), 59–82. Retrieved from ucsf.org/ticr/syllabus/courses/86/2012/11/01/Lecture/readings/How%20many%20interviews%20are%20enough.pdf.

Gupta, A. (2013). "Employee perceptions of managers who express anger: Could a high quality relationship buffer women from backlash?" (doctoral dissertation). Available from ProQuest Dissertations and Theses database. (AAT: 3561786).

Hage-Cameron, S. (2003). *Skill, effort and attitude of teenage female athletes: The relationship to body esteem and self-esteem.* Available from ProQuest Dissertations & Theses database. (UMI No. 305237370).

Hamilton, R. A., D. Scott, & M. P. MacDougall. (2007). "Assessing the effectiveness of self-talk interventions on endurance performance." *Journal of Applied Sport Psychology* 19(2), 226–39. http://dx.doi.org/10.1080/10413200701230613.

Handel, R. (1993). "The contributions of intercollegiate athletic participation on student leadership development." University of Wisconsin-Madison. Retrieved from http://www.worldcat.org/title/contributions-of-intercollegiate-athletic-participation-on-student-leadership-development/oclc/29962649?referer=di&ht=edition

Hatzigeorgiadis, A. (2006). "Instructional and motivational self-talk: An investigation on perceived self-talk functions." *Hellenic Journal of Psychology* 3(2), 164–75. Retrieved from http://www.pseve.org/journal/upload/hatzigeorgiadis3b.pdf.

Hatzigeorgiadis, A., N. Zourbanos, S. Mpoumpaki, & Y. Theodorakis. (2009). "Mechanisms underlying the self-talk–performance relationship: The effects of motivational self-talk on self-confidence and anxiety." *Psychology of Sport and Exercise* 10(1), 186–92. http://dx.doi.org/10.1016/j.psychsport.2008.07.009.

Heilman, M. E. (2001). "Description and prescription: How gender stereotypes prevent women's ascent up the organizational ladder." *Journal of Social Issues* 57, 657–74. http://dx.doi.org/10.1111/0022-4537.00234.

Heilman, M. E., A. S. Wallen, D. Fuchs, & M. Tamkins. (2004). "Penalties for success: Reactions to women who succeed at masculine gender-typed tasks." *Journal of Applied Psychology* 89(3), 416–27. Retrieved from http://psycnet.apa.org/journals/apl/89/3/416/.

Herring, C. (2009). "Does diversity pay? Race, gender, and the business case for diversity." *American Sociological Review* 74, 208–24. Retrieved from http://asr.sagepub.com/content/74/2/208.short.

Hewlett, S. A., C. B. Buck Luce, L. J. Servon, L. Sherbin, P. Shiller, E. Sosnovich, & K. Sumberg.(2008). "The Athena factor: Reversing the brain drain in science, engineering, and technology." *HBR Research Report*. Retrieved from http://documents.library.nsf.gov/edocs/HD6060-. A84-2008-PDF-Athena-factor-Reversing-the-brain-drain-in-science,-engineering,-and-technology.pdf.

Hill, C., C. Corbett, & A. St. Rose. (2010). *Why so few? Women in science, technology, engineering, and mathematics* (AAUW report). Retrieved from http://files.eric.ed.gov/fulltext/ED509653.pdf.

Hirshfield, L. E. (2011). "Authority, expertise, and impression management: Gendered professionalization of chemists in the academy" (doctoral dissertation). Retrieved from http://deepblue. lib.umich.edu/bitstream/handle/2027.42/89796/lhirshf_1. pdf?sequence=1.

Hopkins, M. M., D. A. O'Neil, & D. Bilimoria. (2006). "Effective leadership and successful career advancement: Perspectives from women in health care." *Equal Opportunities International* 25(4), 251–71. Retrieved from www.emeraldinsight.com/0261-0159.htm.

Horwitz, S. K., & I. B. Horwitz. (2007). „The effects of team diversity on team outcomes: A meta-analytic review of team demography." *Journal of Management* 33(6), http://dx.doi. org/10.1177/0149206307308587© 2007.

Howatt, W. A. (2012). *Roles of internal locus of control and self-efficacy on managing job stressors and ryff's six scales of psychological well-being* (Order No. 3517677). Available from ProQuest Dissertations & Theses Global. (1033213457). Retrieved from http://search. proquest.com/docview/1033213457?accountid=34120.

Huppke, R. (2013, August 26). "Diversity fades as you move up the corporate ladder." *Chicago Tribune.* Retrieved from http://articles. chicagotribune.com/2013-08-26/business/ct-biz-0826-wor k-advice-huppke-20130826_1_board-diversity-white-men-man y-diversity-programs.

Hymnowitz, C., & T. D. Schellhardt. (1986, March 24). "The glass ceiling: Why women can't seem to break through the invisible barrier that blocks them from the top jobs." *Wall Street Journal,* 1D, 5D.

Jalbert, T., M. Jalbert, & K. Furumo. (2013). "The relationship between CEO gender, financial performance, and financial management." *Journal of Business & Economics Research* 11(1), 25–33. Retrieved from http://ssrn.com/abstract=2218859.

Jepson, L. J. (2010). *An analysis of factors that influence the success of women engineering leaders in corporate America.* Available from ProQuest Dissertations & Theses database. (UMI No. 193940237).

Jones, M. L. (2007). "Using software to analyse qualitative data." *Malaysian Journal of Qualitative Research* 1(1), 64–76. Retrieved from http://ro.uow.edu.au/cgi/viewcontent. cgi?article=1457&context=commpapers.

Judge, T. A., J. E. Bono, R. Ilies, & M. Werner. (2002). "Personality and leadership: A qualitative and quantitative review." *Journal of Applied Psychology* 87, 765–80. Retrieved from http://psycnet.apa. org/index.cfm?fa=search.displayRecord&uid=2002-15406-013.

Kasper, A. S. (1994). "A feminist, qualitative methodology: A study of women with breast cancer." *Qualitative Sociology* 17(3), 263–81. Retrieved from http://link.springer.com/ article/10.1007%2FBF02422255?LI=true#page-2.

Kauaria, V. (2002). *An investigation of female leaders' perceptions of themselves and their roles as leaders in a Catholic School.* (Master's thesis). Retrieved from http://eprints.ru.ac.za/2029/1/ KAUARIA-MEd-TR03–136.pdf.

Kellett, J. B. (2002). *Empathy, emotional awareness, and task characteristics: A study of leadership perception in small groups.* Available from ProQuest Dissertations & Theses database. (UMI No. 305430482).

Kelsey, K. D. (2007). "Overcoming gender bias with self-efficacy: A case study of women agricultural education teachers and pre-service students." *Journal of Agricultural Education* 48(1), 52–63. Retrieved from http://files.eric.ed.gov/fulltext/EJ840067.pdf.

Koenig, M., A. H. Eagly, A. Mitchell, & T. Ristikari. (2011). "Are leader stereotypes masculine? A meta-analysis of three research paradigms." *Psychological Bulletin* 137(4), 616–42. http://dx.doi. org/10.1037/a0023557.

Kohli, J., J. Gans, & J. Hairston. (2011). *A better, more diverse senior executive service in 2050.* Retrieved from Center for American Progress website: http://www.americanprogress.org/issues/2011/09/pdf/ses_paper.pdf.

Kohlman, M. H. (2004). "Person or position?: The demographics of sexual harassment in the workplace." *Equal Opportunities International* 23(3–5), 143–61. Retrieved from http://search.proquest.com/docview/199537078?accountid=34120.

Kolodinsky, R. W., D. C. Treadway, & G. R. Ferris. (2007). "Political skill and influence effectiveness: Testing portions of an expanded Ferris and Judge (1991) model." *Human Relations* 60(12), 1747–77. http://dx.doi.org/10.1177/0018726707084913.

Komaromy, M., A. B. Bindman, R. J. Haber, & M. A. Sande. (1993). "Sexual harassment in medical training." *New England Journal of Medicine* 328(5), 322–26. http://dx.doi.org/10.1056/NEJM199302043280507.

Landman, M. (2006). "Getting quality in qualitative research: A short introduction to feminist methodology and methods." *Proceedings of the Nutrition Society* 65(04), 429–33. http://dx.doi.org/10.1079/PNS2006518.

LaPierre, T. A., & M. K. Zimmerman. (2012). "Career advancement and gender equity in healthcare management." *Gender in Management* 27(2), 100–118. http://dx.doi.org/10.1108/17542411211214158.

Laud, R. L., & M. Johnson. (2013). "Journey to the top: Are there really gender differences in the selection and utilization of career tactics?" *Journal of Organizational Culture, Communication and Conflict* 17(1), 51–68. Retrieved from https://www.questia.com/library/journal/1P3-3002966161/journey-to-the-top-are-there-really-gender-differences.

Lemons, M. A., & M. Parzinger. (2007). "Gender schemas: A cognitive explanation of discrimination of women in technology." *Journal of Business and Psychology* 22(1), 91–98. http://dx.doi.org/10.1007/s10869-007-9050-0.

Levesque-Lopman, L. (2000). Listen, and you will hear: Reflections on interviewing from a feminist phenomenological perspective."

Feminist Phenomenology 40(2000), 103–32. http://dx.doi. org/10.1007/978-94-015-9488-2_7.

Lewis, J. (2009). "Redefining qualitative methods: Believability in the fifth moment." *International Journal of Qualitative Methods* 8(2). Retrieved from https://ejournals.library.ualberta.ca/index.php/ IJQM/article/view/4408.

Litzky, B., & J. Greenhaus. (2007). "The relationship between gender and aspirations to senior management." *Career Development International* 12(7), 637–59. http://dx.doi.org/10.1108/13620430710834404.

Luster, A. E. (2011). "Narrative experiences of women in a southern state who have achieved the superintendency" (doctoral dissertation). Available from ProQuest Dissertations and Theses database. (AAT: 3472233).

Lyness, K. S., & D. E. Thompson. (2000). "Climbing the corporate ladder: Do female and male executives follow the same route?" *Journal of Applied Psychology* 85(1), 86–101. http://dx.doi. org/10.1037//0021-9010.85.1.86.

Madden, M. (2011). "Gender stereotypes of leaders." *Wagadu 9*. Retrieved from http://appweb.cortland.edu/ojs/index.php/Wagadu/ article/viewFile/638/871.

Madsen, S. R. (2007). "Developing leadership: Exploring childhoods of women university presidents." *Journal of Educational Administration* 45(1), 99–118. http://dx.doi.org/10.1108/09578230710722476.

Maier, M. (1999). "On the gendered substructure of organization: Dimensions and dilemmas of corporate masculinity." In G. Powell (ed.), *Handbook of gender and work*, 69–94). London, England: Sage. Retrieved from http://knowledge.sagepub.com/ view/handbook-of-gender-and-work/n5.xml.

Marla, B. W., & A. N. Smith. (2014). "Importance of women's political skill in male-dominated organizations." *Journal of Managerial Psychology* 29(2), 206–22. http://dx.doi.org/10.1108/JMP-06–2012-0106.

Marsh, D., & P. Furlong. (2002). "A skin not a sweater: Ontology and epistemology in political science." In D. Marsh & G. Stoker (eds.), *Theory and methods in political science* (2ⁿᵈ ed.) 17–21). London, England: Palgrave Macmillan. Retrieved from http://www.palgrave.com/pdfs/0333948556.pdf.

Martin, J. (2003). "Feminist theory and critical theory: Unexplored synergies." *Studying Management Critically*, 66–91. Retrieved from http://csi.gsb.stanford.edu/feminist-theory-critical-theory-unexplored-synergies.

Mason, Mark (2010). "Sample size and saturation in PhD studies using qualitative interviews." *Forum: Qualitative Social Research* 11(3), Art. 8, http://nbn-resolving.de/urn:nbn:de:0114-fqs100387.

Matsa, D., & A. Miller. (2011). "Chipping away at the glass ceiling: Gender spillovers in corporate leadership" [working paper]. Retrieved from http://www.prgs.edu/content/dam/rand/pubs/working_papers/2011/RAND_WR842.pdf.

McLaughlin, H., C. Uggen, & A. Blackstone. (2012). "Sexual harassment, workplace authority, and the paradox of power." *American Sociological Review* 77(4), 625–47. Retrieved from http://search.proquest.com/docview/1032785414?accountid=34120.

Mintzberg, H. (1985). "The organization as political arena." *Journal of Management Studies* 22(2), 133–54. Retrieved from http://web.b.ebscohost.com.proxy.thechicagoschool.edu/ehost/detail?

Monroe, K., S. Ozyurt, T. Wrigley, & A. Alexander. (2008). "Gender equality in academia: Bad news from the trenches, and some possible solutions." *Perspectives on Politics* 6(2), 215–33. Retrieved from http://www.apsanet.org/imgtest/PerspectivesJun08MonroeEtal.pdf.

Moss-Racusin, C. A., & L. A. Rudman. (2010). "Disruptions in women's self-promotion: The backlash avoidance model." *Psychology of Women Quarterly* 34(2), 186–202. Retrieved from http://pwq.sagepub.com/content/34/2/186.

Moustakas, C. (1994). *Phenomenological research methods*. Thousand Oaks, CA: Sage.

National Commission for the Protection of Human Subjects of Biomedical and Behavioral Research. (1979). *Ethical principles and guidelines for the protection of human subjects of research (aka the Belmont Report)*. Retrieved from http://ohsr.od.nih.gov/guidelines/belmont.html.

Noble, C., & S. Moore. (2006). "Advancing women and leadership in this postfeminist, post-EEO era." *Women in Management Review* 21(7), 598–603. http://dx.doi.org/10.1108/09649420610692534.

Oakley, J. G. (2000). "Gender-based barriers to senior management positions: Understanding the scarcity of female CEOs." *Journal of Business Ethics* 27(4), 321–34. http://dx.doi.org/10.1023/A:1006226129868.

Olsson, S., & R. Walker. (2003). "Through a gendered lens? Male and female executives' representations of one another. *Leadership & Organization Development Journal* 24(7), 387–96. Retrieved from http://www.emeraldinsight.com/0143-7739.htm.

———. (2004). "'Two women and the boys': Patterns of identification and differentiation in senior women executives' representations of career identity." *Women in Management Review* 19(5), 244–51. Retrieved from http://search.proquest.com/docview/213193028?

O'Neill, O. A., & C. A. O'Reilly. (2011). "Reducing the backlash effect: Self-monitoring and women's promotions." *Journal of Occupational and Organizational Psychology* 84(4), 825–32. http://dx.doi.org/10.1111/j.2044-8325.2010.02008.x.

Pai, K., & S. Vaidya. (2009). "Glass ceiling: Role of women in the corporate world." *Competitiveness Review* 19(2), 106–13. http://dx.doi.org/10.1108/10595420910942270.

Page, M. C., M. E. Bailey, & J. VanDelinder. (2009). "The blue blazer club: Masculine hegemony in science, technology, engineering, and math fields." *Forum on Public Policy Online* 2. Retrieved from http://www.forumonpublicpolicy.com/summer09/ archivesummer09/page.pdf.

Paris, L. D., & D. L. Decker. (2012). "Sex role stereotypes: Does business education make a difference?" *Gender in Management* 27(1), 36–50. Retrieved from http://www.emeraldinsight.com/journals. htm?articleid=17014415&show=abstract.

Pascale, R., J. Sternin, & M. Sternin. (2010). *The power of positive deviance.* Boston: Harvard Business School. Retrieved from http://www. pwrnewmedia.com/2011/nortonnorris/newsletter/winter2012/ downloads/PositiveDeviance.pdf.

Patton, M. Q., & M. Cochran. (2002). *A guide to using qualitative research methodology.* Retrieved from *Medicins sans Frontiers* website: http:// fieldresearch.msf.org/msf/bitstream/10144/84230/1/Qualitative research methodology.pdf.

Peshkin, A. (1988, October). "In search of subjectivity—one's own." *Educational Researcher* 17(7), 17–21. Retrieved from http://h1213. pbworks.com/w/file/fetch/58510211.

Ponterotto, J. G. (2005). "Qualitative research in counseling psychology: A primer on research paradigms and philosophy of science." *Journal of Counseling Psychology* 52(2), 126–36. http://dx.doi. org/10.1037/0022-0167.52.2.126.

Randolph, J. (2009). "A guide to writing the dissertation literature review." *Practical Assessment, Research & Evaluation* 14(13). Retrieved from http://pareonline.net/getvn.asp?v=14&n=13.

Reinhold, B. (2005). "Smashing glass ceilings: Why women still find it tough to advance to the executive suite." *Journal of Organizational Excellence* 24, 43–55. http://dx.doi.org/10.1002/joe. 20054.

Richman, L. S., M. van Dellen, & W. Wood. (2011). "How women cope: Being a numerical minority in a male-dominated profession." *Journal of Social Issues* 67, 492–509. http://dx.doi. org/10.1111/j.1540–4560.2011.01711.x.

Ridgeway, C. L. (2009). "Framed before we know it: How gender shapes social relations." *Gender & Society* 23(2), 145–60. Retrieved from http://gas.sagepub.com/content/23/2/145.short.

Rose, M. W., & S. Thomas. (2009). "Workplace Culture that hinders and assists the career development of women in information technology." *Learning and Performance Journal* 25(1), 25–42. Retrieved from http://search.proquest.com/docview/219817356?accountid=34120 in organizations.

Rosenberg, G. N. (2004). "The 1964 Civil Rights Act: The crucial role of social movements in the enactment and implementation of anti-discrimination law." *St. Louis University Law Journal* 49, 1147–54. Retrieved from http://chicagounbound.uchicago.edu/cgi/viewcontent.cgi?article=2924&context=journal_articles.

Rosenthal, P. (1995). "Gender differences in managers' attributions for successful work performance." *Women in Management Review* 10(6), 26. Retrieved from http://search.proquest.com/docview/213148331?accountid=34120.

Rowe, M. (1990). "Barriers to equality: The power of subtle discrimination to maintain unequal opportunity." *Employee Responsibilities and Rights Journal* 3(2), 153–63. Retrieved from http://web.mit.edu/ombuds/publications/barriers.pdf.

Rudman, L. A., & K. Fairchild. (2004). "Reactions to counterstereotypic behavior: The role of backlash in cultural stereotype maintenance." *Journal of Personality and Social Psychology* 87(2), 157–76. http://dx.doi.org/10.1037/0022-3514.87.2.157.

Rudman, L. A., & P. Glick. (2001). "Prescriptive gender stereotypes and backlash toward agentic women." *Journal of Social Issues* 57, 732–62. Retrieved from http://edutexts.org/tw_files2/urls_57/108/d-107003/7z-docs/217.pdf.

———. (1999). "Feminized management and backlash toward agentic women: The hidden costs to women of a kinder, gentler image of middle managers." *Journal of Personality and Social Psychology* 77(5), 1004–10. http://dx.doi.org/10.1037/0022–3514.77.5.1004.

Rudman, L. A., C. A. Moss-Racusin, J. E. Phelan, & S. Nauts. (2012). "Status incongruity and backlash effects: Defending the gender hierarchy motivates prejudice against female leaders." *Journal of Experimental Social Psychology* 48(1), 165–79. http://dx.doi.org/10.1016/j.jesp.2011.10.008.

Rudman, L. A., & J. E. Phelan. (2008). "Backlash effects for disconfirming gender stereotypes in organizations." *Research in Organizational Behavior* 28(2008), 61–79. http://dx.doi.org/10.1016/j.riob.2008.04.003.

Ryan, F., M. Coughlan, & P. Cronin. (2007). "Step-by-step guide to critiquing research. Part 2: Qualitative research." *British Journal of Nursing* 16(12), 738–45. Retrieved from http://keiranhenderson.com/articulate/Critiquing_research/data/downloads/critiquing_qualitative_research_bjn.pdf.

Saldaña, J. (2012). *The coding manual for qualitative researchers* (14). Thousand Oaks, CA: Sage.

Schein, V. E. (1973). "The relationship between sex role stereotypes and requisite management characteristics." *Journal of Applied Psychology* 57(2), 95–100. Retrieved from http://psycnet.apa.org/journals/apl/60/3/340/.

Schein, V. E., & M. J. Davidson. (1993). "Think manager, think male." *Management Development Review* 6(3), 24. http://dx.doi.org/10.1108/EUM0000000000738.

Schipani, C. A., T. M. Dworkin, A. Kwolek-Folland, & V. G. Maurer. (2009). "Pathways for women to obtain positions of organizational leadership: The significance of mentoring and networking. *Duke Journal of Gender Law and Policy* 16, 89–136. Retrieved from http://deepblue.lib.umich.edu/bitstream/handle/2027.42/61158/1117_CSchipani.pdf&embedded=true?sequence=1.

Schneider, B. (1987). "The people make the place." *Personnel psychology* 40(3), 437–53. Retrieved from http://misweb.cbi.msstate.edu/~COBI/faculty/users/jvardaman/files/autoweb/MGT811101oncampus/Schneider1987.pdf.

Seidel, J. V. (1998). "Qualitative data analysis." *Qualis Research, Appendix E,"* Retrieved from http://www.qualisresearch.com/DownLoads/qda.pdf.

Seidman, I. (2013). *Interviewing as qualitative research: A guide for researchers in education and the social sciences.* New York: Teachers College Press.

Shaughnessy, B. A., D. C. Treadway, J. A. Breland, L. V. Williams, & R. L. Brouer. (2011). "Influence and promotability: The importance of female political skill." *Journal of Managerial Psychology* 26(7), 584–603. http://dx.doi.org/10.1108/02683941111164490.

Sheridan, A., & G. Milgate. (2003). "'She says, he says': Women's and men's views of the composition of boards." *Women in Management Review* 18(3), 147. Retrieved from http://www.emeraldinsight.com/journals.htm?articleid=1412262&show=abstract.

Shivers-Blackwell, S. (2006). "The influence of perceptions of organizational structure and culture on leadership role requirements: The moderating impact of locus of control & self-monitoring." *Journal of Leadership & Organizational Studies* 12(4), 27–49. http://dx.doi.org/10.1177/107179190601200403.

Sikdar, A., & S. Mitra. (2009). "An exploration of gender stereotypes in perception and practice of leadership." In 9th Global Conference on Business and Economics. Cambridge, UK: Cambridge University Press. Retrieved from http://www.gcbe.us/9th_GCBE/data/confcd.htm.

Simmons, A. L., J. A. Duffy, & H. S. Alfraih. (2012). "Attitudes toward women managers: The influence of social dominance orientation and power distance on men in college." *Gender in Management: An International Journal* 27(7), 482–98. Retrieved from http://www.ingentaconnect.com/content/mcb/gm/2012/00000027/00000007/art00004.

Singh, V., S. Kumra, & S. Vinnicombe. (2002). "Gender and impression management: Playing the promotion game." *Journal of Business Ethics* 37(1), 77. Retrieved from http://search.proquest.com/docview/198056866?accountid=34120.

Skinner, J. L. (2006). "Women's pursuit of advancement opportunities: The impact of gendered climates on women's perceptions of fit with leadership" (doctoral dissertation). Available from ProQuest Dissertations and Theses database. (AAT: 3227660).

Smith, S. L. (2010). "Implications of gender stereotypes for public policy" (doctoral dissertation). Available from ProQuest Dissertations and Theses database. (AAT: 3403982).

Smith, P., P. Caputi, & N. Crittenden. (2012). "A maze of metaphors around glass ceilings." *Gender in Management* 27(7), 436–48. http://dx.doi.org/10.1108/17542411211273432.

Soares, R. (2012). *2012 catalyst census: Fortune 500 women executive officers and top earners*. Appendix 6: Companies with zero women executive officers. Retrieved from Catalyst website: http://www.catalyst.org/knowledge/2012-catalyst-census-fortune–500-women-executive-officers-and-top-earners.

Soe, L., & E. K. Yakura. (2008). "What's wrong with the pipeline? Assumptions about gender and culture in IT work." *Women Studies Journal* 37(3), 176–201. Retrieved from http://www.tandfonline.com/doi/pdf/10.1080/00497870801917028.

Sörlin, A., A. Ohman, Y. Blomstedt, H. Stenlund, and L. Lindholm. (2011). "Measuring the gender gap in organizations." *Gender in Management: An International Journal* 26, 275–88. http://dx.doi.org/10.1108/17542411111144292.

Steinke, J. (2013). "In her own voice: Identity centrality and perceptions of workplace climate in blogs by women scientists." *International Journal of Gender, Science and Technology* 5(1), 25–51. Retrieved from http://genderandset.open.ac.uk/index.php/genderandset/article/viewArticle/264.

Svara, J. H. (2003). "Two decades of continuity and change in American city councils." *Commission by the National League of Cities.* Retrieved from http://www.skidmore.edu/~bturner/Svara citycouncilrpt.pdf.

Thorne, S. (2000). "Data analysis in qualitative research." *Evidence Based Nursing* 3, 68–70. Retrieved from http://ebn.bmj.com/content/3/3/68.full.

Todd, S. Y., K. J. Harris, R. B. Harris, & A. R. Wheeler. (2009). "Career success implications of political skill." *Journal of Social Psychology* 149(3), 179–304. http://dx.doi.org/10.3200/SOCP.149.3.279-304.

Tufford, L., & P. Newman. (2012). "Bracketing in qualitative research." *Qualitative Social Work* 11(1), 80–96. http://dx.doi.org/10.1177/1473325010368316.

Uggen, C., & A. Blackstone. (2004). "Sexual harassment as a gendered expression of power." *American Sociological Review* 69(1), 64–92. http://dx.doi.org/10.1177/000312240406900105.

Van Manen, M. (1977). "Linking ways of knowing with ways of being practical." *Curriculum Inquiry* 6(3), 205–28. Retrieved from http://www.jstor.org/stable/1179579.

Van Manen, M. (1984). "'Doing' phenomenological research and writing: An introduction." *Monograph No. 7, Curriculum Praxis,* 1–29. Retrieved from http://www2.education.ualberta.ca/educ/sec/docs/MonographNo.7-vanManen.pdf.

Vendrik, M. C. M., & C. Schwieren. (2010). "Identification, screening, and stereotyping in labour market discrimination." *Journal of Economics* 99(2), 141–71. http://dx.doi.org/10.1007/s00712-009-0106-7.

Vinnicombe, S. (2011). "Reflections on 'locks and keys to the boardroom.'" *Gender in Management: An International Journal* 26, 196–99. http://dx.doi.org/10.1108/17542411111130954.

Von Hellens, L.A., S. H. Nielsen, E. M. Trauth. (2001). "Breaking and entering the male domain: Women in the IT industry." *Proceedings of the ACM SIGMIS Conference on Computer Personnel Research.* (San Diego, April): 116–20. Retrieved from http://freepdfs.net/breakin g-and-entering-the-male-domain-women-in-the-it-industry/ eaded4d62685d5e9a1cf13a3408da1b4/.

Watts, Jacqueline H. (2009). "Leaders of men: Women 'managing' in construction." *Work, Employment and Society* 23(3), 512–30. Retrieved from http://wes.sagepub.com/content/23/3/512.

Watson, W., K. Kumar, & K. Michaelsen. (1993). "Cultural diversity's impact on interaction process and performance: Comparing homogeneous and diverse task groups." *Academy of Management Journal* 36(3), 590–602. Retrieved from http://amj.aom.org/ content/36/3/590.short.

Weele, B., & M. E. Heilman. (2005). "Formal and informal discrimination against women at work: The role of gender stereotypes." In D. Steiner, S. Gilliland, & D. Skarlicki (eds.), *Research in social issues in management: Managing social and ethical issues in organizations.* Retrieved fromhttp://dspace.mit.edu/bitstream/ handle/1721.1/55933/CPL_WP_5_2_HeilmanWelle.pdf.

Weiss, A. M., N. H. Lurie, & D. J. MacInnis. (2008). "Listening to strangers: Whose responses are valuable, how valuable are they, and why?" *Journal of Marketing Research* 45(4), 425–36. Retrieved from http://journals.ama.org/doi/abs/10.1509/jmkr.45.4.425.

Welbourne, T. M., C. S. Cycyota, & C. J. Ferrante. (2007). "Wall Street reaction to women in IPOs: An examination of gender diversity in top management teams." *Group & Organization Management* 32(5), 524–47. http://dx.doi.org/10.1177/1059601106291071.

Welsch, E. (2002). "Dealing with Data: Using NVivo in the Qualitative Data Analysis Process." *Qualitative Social Research* 3(2), Art. 26. Retrieved from http://nbn-resolving.de/ urn:nbn:de:0114-fqs0202260.

Wentling, R. M., & S. Thomas. (2009). "Workplace culture that hinders and assists the career development of women in information technology." *Information Technology, Learning, and Performance Journal* 25(1), 25–42. Retrieved from http://connection.ebscohost.com/c/articles/46800519/workplace-culture-that-hinders-assists-career-development-women-information-technology.

Wertz, F. J. (2005). "Phenomenological research methods for counseling psychology." *Journal of Counseling Psychology* 52(2), 167–77. Retrieved from http://www.grad.umn.edu/prod/groups/grad/@pub/@grad/documents/asset/wertz_fj (2008).pdf.

Weyer, B. (2007). "Twenty years later: Explaining the persistence of the glass ceiling for women leaders." *Women in Management Review* 22(6), 482–96. Retrieved from http://www.emeraldinsight.com/journals.htm?articleid=1621633.

Whiting, L. (2002). "Analysis of phenomenological data: Personal reflections on Giorgi's method." *Nurse Researcher* 9(2), 60–74. Retrieved from http://dx.doi.org/10.7748/nr2002.01.9.2.60.c6183.

Whyte, W. H. (1956). *The organization man.* Delran, NJ: Simon & Schuster.

Wickham, M., & M. Woods. (2005). "Reflecting on the strategic use of CAQDAS to manage and report on the qualitative research process." *Qualitative Report* 10(4), 687–702. Retrieved from http://www.nova.edu/ssss/QR/QR10-4/wickham.pdf.

Woolf, V. (1945). *A Room of One's Own.* Penguin Books, London.

"Women Presidents or Chancellors of Co-ed Colleges and Universities." (2014, July 10). In *Wikipedia, the Free Encyclopedia.* Retrieved July 22, 2014, from http://en.wikipedia.org/w/index.php?title=Women_Presidents_or_Chancellors_of_Co-ed_Colleges_and_Universities&oldid=616378611.

Wordsworth, W. (1888). *The Complete Poetical Works.* London: Macmillan. Retrieved from www.bartleby.com/145/.

Zajac, E. J., & J. D. Westphal. (1996). „Who shall succeed? How CEO/ Board preferences and power affect the choice of new CEOs." *Academy of Management Journal*, 39(1), 64–90. Retrieved from http://www.jstor.org/stable/256631.

Zeiler, K., & L. F. Käll (eds.). (2014). *Feminist phenomenology and medicine.* New York: State University of New York Press.

Zourbanos, N., A. Papaioannou, E. Argyropoulou, & A. Hatzigeorgiadis. (2014). "Achievement goals and self-talk in physical education: The moderating role of perceived competence." *Motivation and Emotion* 38(2), 235–51. http://dx.doi.org/10.1007/s11031-013–9378-x.

APPENDIX A

Interview Protocol
and Questions

Interview Protocol

The researcher will conduct face-to-face in-depth interviews consisting of open-ended questions guided by the research questions. The researcher will be flexible enough to allow for the exploration of additional factors or issues that may emerge and that encourage narration of the participant's stories and experiences. Free listing is an interview technique that can help to identify important themes that lead to the essence of the phenomenon. In free listing, the researcher asks participants to identify all the factors or issues that contributed to their experiences of overcoming gender discrimination and then to discuss these experiences according to importance or significance (Patton & Cochran 2002). Another phenomenological interviewing approach asks the participant to recall critical incidents, turning points, or significant decisions that may have been a result of the phenomenon under study (Patton & Cochran 2002). The researcher may schedule additional interviews that contain probing follow-up questions to ensure that a comprehensive examination of the participant's lived experience takes place.

The researcher will utilize a script that begins with an explanation of the study and a request for the participant's consent. The researcher will provide a consent form to each participant, and interviewing will not begin until the participant reads and signs the consent form and returns it to the researcher. Interviews will take place in quiet, private, and distraction-free environments. The researcher will audio-record all interviews. The researcher will interview all participants on two to three occasions for approximately ninety minutes each session and record the interviews with the permission of the participant. After the interviews, the researcher will transcribe the recordings verbatim and house the transcripts in confidential computer files. The researcher will make daily backups of the files. The researcher will take all appropriate precautions to ensure that neither the participant nor her company will be identifiable in any report. Throughout the study, the researcher will be highly cognizant of potential ethical issues and/or harm to subjects and will employ all appropriate procedures to minimize the risks. Since the primary data collection instrument in qualitative research is the researcher, it is essential that she accurately record the experiences, reflections, insights, and observations research participants share (Lewis, 2009).

Interview Questions

Career History

1. What was your first professional position in STEM, and how did you get that job?

2. What significant experiences or people do you recall from that first job?

3. What impact did these experiences and/or people have on you?

4. What were the greatest challenges you encountered?

5. What made these situations particularly challenging, and what did you do?

6. What was the best coaching that you received in the early stages of your career?

7. What did you discover about yourself that best equipped you for leadership in the male-dominated STEM profession?

8. What was the next step for you in your career? How did that come about? (Continue until participant comes to present position.)

9. As you reflect on your career journey, how has it shaped you? Are there any situations or experiences that were most influential in shaping your behavior?

Career Experiences

1. What is it like to be a female leader in STEM?

2. Please describe in as much detail as possible a situation in which you experienced gender bias or backlash that blocked your career or academic advancement.

   a. What was it like for you to be in that situation?

   b. What effect has that had on your life and your career?

3. Please describe in as much detail as possible an experience in which you consciously chose behaviors to mitigate the impact of gender bias on your career advancement.

   a. What was it like for you to do that?

b.   What effect has that had on your life and your career?

4.   How is the path to senior leadership different for women in STEM than for men?

5.   What are the greatest barriers to women in STEM who wish to achieve positions of senior leadership?

6.   What experiences, insights, or knowledge were most helpful in preparing you for a senior leadership position in STEM?

7.   What personal traits, beliefs, skills, or strategies contributed to your success in the traditionally male-dominated field of STEM?

8.   In what ways did self-confidence enable you to attain your senior leadership position?

9.   In what ways did self-monitoring (explain) strategies enable you to attain your senior leadership position?

10. In what ways did political skills enable you to attain your senior leadership position?

11. What other buffering behaviors (explain) enabled you to attain your senior leadership position?

12. What would you have done differently, if anything, on your journey to senior leadership in STEM?

13. How did you demonstrate that you were competent and capable of holding a senior leadership position in STEM?

14. What do you know now about achieving senior leadership in STEM that you wish you had known earlier in your career?

15. What advice would you offer to other women who wish to follow in your footsteps?

16. Are there any other experiences that you have had on your journey to leadership that we have not discussed that have been significant and, if so, would you tell me about them?

Follow-up probes.

A. You mentioned _____. Would you tell me more about that?

B. You mentioned _____. What was that like for you?

C. How did you respond?

D. Would you respond differently now? In what ways?

Closing

1. Is there anything you would like to discuss in more depth?

2. Would you like to share any final thoughts, reflections, or advice before our interview concludes?

APPENDIX B

Participant Screening Questionnaire

The purpose of this study is to discover how women who are leaders in the fields of science, technology, engineering, and mathematics (STEM) have overcome gender-based barriers to reach senior level leadership positions in their organizations.

Please answer the following questions by checking either Yes _____ or No _____.

1. Have you encountered any gender-based challenges, obstacles, or barriers in your career?

    Yes_____ No_____

2. When confronted with gender-based barriers, have you used certain behaviors that helped you overcome these obstacles?

    Yes_____ No_____

3. Could you give examples of any specific behaviors you have found effective in overcoming gender-based barriers?

    Yes_____ No_____

Thank you.